Exam Ref MS-500
Microsoft 365 Security
Administration

Ed Fisher
Nate Chamberlain

Exam Ref MS-500 Microsoft 365 Security Administration

Published with the authorization of Microsoft Corporation by
Pearson Education, Inc.

ISBN-13: 978-0-13-580264-9
ISBN-10: 0-13-580264-4

Library of Congress Control Number: 2020942705

1 2020

TRADEMARKS

WARNING AND DISCLAIMER

SPECIAL SALES

For information about buying this title in bulk quantities, or for special sales op-
portunities (which may include electronic versions; custom cover designs; and
content particular to your business, training goals, marketing focus, or branding
interests), please contact our corporate sales department at corpsales@pearsoned.
com or (800) 382-3419.

For government sales inquiries, please contact governmentsales@pearsoned.com.

For questions about sales outside the U.S., please contact intlcs@pearson.com.

CREDITS

EDITOR-IN-CHIEF
Brett Bartow

EXECUTIVE EDITOR
Loretta Yates

SPONSORING EDITOR
Charvi Arora

DEVELOPMENT EDITOR
Rick Kughen

MANAGING EDITOR
Sandra Schroeder

PROJECT EDITOR
Tracey Croom

COPY EDITOR
Rick Kughen

INDEXER
Cheryl Lenser

PROOFREADER
Sarah Kearns

TECHNICAL EDITORS
Ed Fisher, Bryan Lesko

EDITORIAL ASSISTANT
Cindy Teeters

COVER DESIGNER
Twist Creative, Seattle

GRAPHICS
TJ Graham Art

I dedicate this book to my wife, Connie, without whom this could not have happened and would not have mattered. Thanks for being my better half in every way. And to my fellow TSs with whom I share the best role at Microsoft.

—ED FISHER

Contents at a glance

Contents

Chapter 4   Manage governance and compliance features in Microsoft 365   131

About the Authors

Ed Fisher, Security & Compliance Architect at Microsoft, focuses on all aspects of security and compliance within Office 365, especially Microsoft Threat Protection. He has spent nearly a decade helping Microsoft customers and partners succeed with Microsoft cloud and productivity solutions. You can learn more at *https://aka.ms/edfisher*.

Nate Chamberlain is a Microsoft 365 Certified Enterprise Administrator Expert. He has been an Office Apps and Services MVP since 2019, frequently blogging at *NateChamberlain.com* and speaking at Microsoft-focused events and user groups.

Acknowledgments

I'd like to express my deep gratitude to the following people, without whom this book would not have been possible.

Thank you to Loretta for bringing me into this project. Your patience is greatly appreciated! Thank you, Rick, for painstakingly editing every corner of this book to make it a better reading experience. Thanks to Bryan for all the early work and assistance. Thanks to Nate for coming in at the eleventh hour to bring this thing home. Thanks to Charvi for taking care of all the details that keep everything on track. Thanks to Greg for greenlighting this side hustle. Finally, thank you to all the people at Microsoft Press who worked so hard to create this book from the digital manuscript.

—Ed Fisher

I'm grateful to the hard-working team behind this book who brought me on board with Ed to write this guide and continually helped us make it the best it can be all the way to the press. Professional and personal growth are dear topics to me, and it's an honor of mine to be able to be part of this project, ultimately helping tech professionals gain their next certifications.

I also want to acknowledge the amazingly supportive and encouraging MVP community, as well as everyone out there who attends local and larger conferences and gets involved in user groups and professional networks. Time is always in short supply, and energy is limited. Making the decision to spend both time and energy in pursuit of community and growth is commendable, and I wish you the best in your ongoing endeavors.

—Nate Chamberlain

Introduction

The purpose of the MS-500 exam is to test your comprehension and practical ability when working with security and compliance features across Microsoft 365 and Azure. The exam includes high-level concepts that apply across all of Microsoft 365 to important concepts that are specific to a particular app or service. Like the exam, this book is geared toward giving you a broad understanding of Microsoft 365 Security Administration, as well as many common services and components on a more granular level.

While we've made every effort possible to make the information in this book accurate, Microsoft 365 is rapidly evolving, and there's a chance that some of the screens shown are slightly different now than they were when this book was written. It's also possible that other minor changes have taken place, such as minor name changes in features and so on.

This book covers every major topic area found on the exam, but it does not cover every exam question. Only the Microsoft exam team has access to the exam questions, and Microsoft regularly adds new questions to the exam, making it impossible to cover specific questions. You should consider this book a supplement to your relevant real-world experience and other study materials. In many cases, we've provided links in the "More Info" sections of the book, and these links are a great source for additional study.

Organization of this book

This book is organized by the "Skills measured" list published for the exam. The "Skills measured" list is available for each exam on the Microsoft Learning website: *http://aka.ms/examlist*. Each chapter in this book corresponds to a major topic area in the list, and the technical tasks in each topic area determine a chapter's organization. Because the MS-500 exam covers four major topic areas, this book contains four chapters.

Preparing for the exam

Microsoft certification exams are a great way to build your resume and let the world know about your level of expertise. Certification exams validate your on-the-job experience and product knowledge. Although there is no substitute for on-the-job experience, preparation through study and hands-on practice can help you prepare for the exam. We recommend that you augment your exam preparation plan by using a combination of available study materials and courses. For example, you might use the Exam Ref and another study guide for your "at home" preparation and take a Microsoft Official Curriculum course for the classroom experience. Choose the combination that you think works best for you.

Note that this Exam Ref is based on publicly available information about the exam and the authors' experiences. To safeguard the integrity of the exam, authors do not have access to the live exam.

Microsoft certifications

Microsoft certifications distinguish you by proving your command of a broad set of skills and experience with current Microsoft products and technologies. The exams and corresponding certifications are developed to validate your mastery of critical competencies as you design and develop, or implement and support, solutions with Microsoft products and technologies both on-premises and in the cloud. Certification brings a variety of benefits to the individual and to employers and organizations.

> **MORE INFO**   **ALL MICROSOFT CERTIFICATIONS**
>
> For information about Microsoft certifications, including a full list of available certifications, go to *http://www.microsoft.com/learn*.

Quick access to online references

Throughout this book are addresses to webpages that the authors have recommended you visit for more information. Some of these links can be very long and painstaking to type, so we've shortened them for you to make them easier to visit. We've also compiled them into a single list that readers of the print edition can refer to while they read.

Download the list at *https://MicrosoftPressStore.com/ExamRefMS500/downloads*.

The URLs are organized by chapter and heading. Every time you come across a URL in the book, find the hyperlink in the list to go directly to the webpage.

Errata, updates, & book support

We've made every effort to ensure the accuracy of this book and its companion content. You can access updates to this book—in the form of a list of submitted errata and their related corrections—at *MicrosoftPressStore.com/ExamRefMS500/errata*.

If you discover an error that is not already listed, please submit it to us at the same page.

For additional book support and information, please visit *https://MicrosoftPressStore.com/Support*.

Please note that product support for Microsoft software and hardware is not offered through the previous addresses. For help with Microsoft software or hardware, go to *http://support.microsoft.com*.

Stay in touch

Let's keep the conversation going! We're on Twitter: *http://twitter.com/MicrosoftPress*.

Implement and manage identity and access

Microsoft 365 identity and access topics are at the core of everything you'll review in this book as you prepare for taking the MS-500 exam. Before any monitoring, reports, policies, compliance, governance, and so on can be optimally effective, an organization must have a firm grasp on how their users are set up in Azure AD, what authentication methods and scenarios are allowed, and which tools at their disposal will be used to enhance their security, such as Azure AD Privileged Identity Management (PIM). In this chapter, we'll cover all these topics in the order of the exam's skills listed below.

Skills in this chapter:

- Skill 1.1: Secure Microsoft 365 hybrid environments
- Skill 1.2: Secure identities
- Skill 1.3: Implement authentication methods
- Skill 1.4: Implement conditional access
- Skill 1.5: Implement role-based access control (RBAC)
- Skill 1.6: Implement Azure AD Privileged Identity Management (PIM)
- Skill 1.7: Implement Azure AD Identity Protection

Skill 1.1: Secure Microsoft 365 hybrid environments

Securing your Microsoft 365 hybrid environments involves understanding and implementing the appropriate Azure AD authentication and synchronization options for your specific scenario, as well as knowing how to monitor and troubleshoot Azure AD Connect events.

This skill covers how to:
- Plan Azure AD authentication options
- Plan Azure AD synchronization options
- Monitor and troubleshoot Azure AD Connect events

Plan Azure AD authentication options

One of the first decisions you'll be making when configuring a Microsoft 365 hybrid environment is which Azure AD authentication method you'll utilize. You have three options to consider:

- Password hash synchronization (PHS)
- Pass-through authentication (PTA)
- Federation (AD FS)

PHS and PTA provide the benefit of seamless single sign-on (SSO) for employees connecting from a corporate or domain-joined device on your network, whereas AD FS cannot.

Method	Distinctions
Password hash synchronization (PHS)	<ul><li>Simplest to deploy.</li><li>No additional infrastructure required.</li><li>Users use the same username/password as on-premises.</li><li>Some premium features in AAD require PHS, such as Identity Protection, which is covered later in this chapter.</li><li>Password hashes are stored in the cloud.</li></ul>
Pass-through authentication (PTA)	<ul><li>Requires password agent installation on server(s).</li><li>Password validation happens on-premises.</li><li>Best for organizations that require on-premises authentication.</li></ul>
Federation (AD FS)	<ul><li>AAD relies on another authentication system.</li><li>Ideal when smartcards, certificates, or third-party multifactor authentication (MFA) are required.</li></ul>

You might end up deploying more than one method, such as PTA with PHS, to be able to benefit from some of the AAD premium features that require PHS.

EXAM TIP **PASSWORD HASH SYNCHRONIZATION (PHS)**

Remember that without PHS enabled, you cannot utilize premium features in Azure AD, such as Identity Protection's leaked credentials detection report.

Plan Azure AD synchronization options

Syncing data between Azure AD and your on-premises Active Directory is handled by the on-premises component Azure AD Connect Sync (or sync engine) working with the service component in Azure AD called Azure AD Connect Sync Service.

When you install Azure AD Connect, you can stick with the default Express settings, which include the following capabilities for single-AD forest setups:

- Configure sync of identities in the current AD forest
- Configure PHS from on-premises AD to Azure AD
- Start initial synchronization upon completion

- Synchronize all attributes
- Enable Auto Upgrade

You'll then navigate through the installation wizard. You'll be prompted to sign in to Azure AD as a Global Administrator, and then you'll sign in to your on-premises Active Directory Domain Services (AD DS) Enterprise Administrator account.

If you choose to customize the settings instead of using the Express settings, you can choose to change the sign-in method from PHS to PTA, Federation with AD FS, Federation with PingFederate, or None. You can also enable or disable Single Sign-On for corporate device users. Read the documentation on these options at *https://docs.microsoft.com/en-us/azure/ active-directory/hybrid/how-to-connect-install-custom#user-sign-in*.

Other customizations you can consider include user and attribute filtering to keep certain identities and data from syncing, and allowing password, group, and/or device writeback for Azure AD–created or modified assets that are syncing back down to your on-premises directory.

EXAM TIP **EXPRESS SETTINGS IN AZURE AD CONNECT INSTALLATION**

If the exam mentions Azure AD Connect being configured using "default authentication settings," that's referring to these "Express settings" that are selected by default and listed above.

Monitor and troubleshoot Azure AD Connect events

In the Azure portal (*https://portal.azure.com*), you can find Azure Active Directory Connect Health with some settings to help make monitoring and troubleshooting Azure AD Connect events simpler. For example, email notifications are enabled by default, but you can add additional recipients.

Azure AD Connect Health helps you identify and manage:

- Email notifications
- Failed sign-ins
- ADFS system issues
- Quick agent installation
- Auto upgrades
- Top application usage
- Network locations and TCP connections

For example, you might receive an "Unhealthy Identity Synchronization" email notification. This is usually the result of the server on which you've installed Azure AD Connect being offline or that your credentials are invalid. Check the server connectivity status to make sure it can access the Azure AD service and be sure your subscription's license for AAD is valid with the credentials you've used to configure it.

You can explore all that's possible using Azure Active Directory Connect Health by reviewing the official documentation located at *https://docs.microsoft.com/en-us/azure/active-directory/hybrid/whatis-azure-ad-connect#what-is-azure-ad-connect-health*.

You can also monitor and troubleshoot Azure AD Connect sync events by using the Event Viewer app's application event log on the server on which you've installed Azure AD Connect sync. Azure AD Connect events are logged and found by navigating to **Event Viewer** > **Windows Logs** > **Application**, as shown in Figure 1-1.

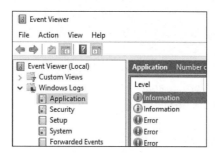

FIGURE 1-1   Using the Event Viewer navigation pane to access Application logs

You may also use the Azure AD Connect Health Sync errors page to help troubleshoot and resolve specific sync errors. Sync errors can be found directly at *https://portal.azure.com/#blade/Microsoft_Azure_ADHybridHealth/AadHealthMenuBlade/SyncErrors* or by searching for **connect health** from the Azure portal and selecting **Sync Errors**, as shown in Figure 1-2.

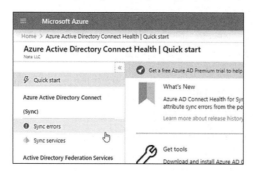

FIGURE 1-2   The Azure AD Connect Health navigation pane in the Azure portal

In many cases, you can run the Azure AD Connect installation wizard again to see if any error messages come up, such as discovering a sync is being attempted. To stop a sync so that you can make configuration changes, you can open the Synchronization Service Manager and manually stop the sync in progress. Then you can run the wizard again to make changes.

There are many more potential errors that could occur during synchronization than will be covered in the exam or this book, but you can read more about possibilities with suggested resolutions at *https://docs.microsoft.com/en-us/azure/active-directory/hybrid/tshoot-connect-sync-errors*.

Skill 1.2: Secure identities

This skill will cover the configuration and management of identity topics around group memberships and the administration that goes into keeping them current and their members secure.

> **This skill covers how to:**
> - Implement Azure AD group membership
> - Implement password management
> - Configure and manage identity governance

Implement Azure AD group membership

Groups in Azure Active Directory can be created as static (assigned) membership groups where someone must manually add new members, or they can be created as automatic (dynamic) groups in which membership is granted based on user or device properties. For example, you could have a human resources dynamic group that automatically includes anybody whose department name includes "human resources."

To create a group, navigate to Azure AD (*https://portal.azure.com*) and then choose **Active Directory** > **Groups** > **New Group**.

You can create one of two group types:

- **Security.** Can be used to grant permissions to shared resources in Office 365 and to apply policies to members.
- **Office 365.** Can be used to grant access to shared collaboration resources, such as Teams, SharePoint sites, shared mailboxes, and the like. This group type also requires that you create an email alias for the group.

Membership for the group can be one of two Office 365 group types:

- **Assigned.** You (or a group owner or other admin) manually declare who is part of the group.
- **Dynamic User.** You define the parameters of user properties for accounts that will be included automatically.

Security groups have an additional option for membership type:

- **Dynamic Device.** Define the parameters of device properties for devices that will be included automatically.

For Dynamic groups, you'll add expressions that define the properties of accounts to be included. See Figure 1-3 for an example of rules being configured.

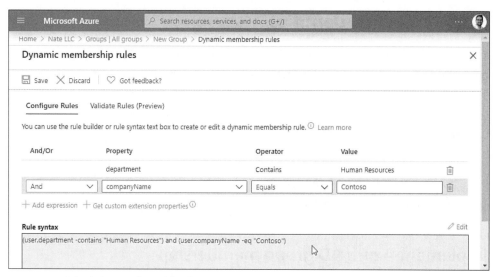

FIGURE 1-3 Rules being configured for dynamic membership in an Azure AD group

Implement password management

Allowing users to reset their passwords saves time for the IT administrative staff and gets us-ers back to work quickly, no matter where or when they're working. Azure AD has self-service password reset (SSPR) you can deploy to all users or only to a specific security group of users.

To enable SSPR, select **Password Reset** from the Azure AD navigation menu, and then choose to whom the SSPR ability should be granted:

- **All.** Everyone in your organization is granted SSPR.
- **Selected.** Specify a single security group.
- **None.** No one is granted SSPR.

This setting only applies to your organization's users because admins always have SSPR and use two factors to reset their passwords when required.

Configure and manage identity governance

Identity governance in Azure AD involves regularly analyzing and confirming or cleaning up group memberships. You can use access reviews to have users confirm their own continued need for their group memberships, or you can assign Access Reviews to individuals responsible for the group memberships. Either way, the user or group reviewer will receive an email with a link that takes him or her to a review page where continued membership can be confirmed or denied (for themselves or for those they're reviewing).

To get started, you must have Azure AD Premium P2 licensing. Then go to Azure AD and select **Identity Governance** from the navigation menu and then select **Access Reviews** > **New Access Review**.

There are several things you must configure when setting up a new access review, as you can see in the example shown in Figure 1-4, including:

- **Review Name.** The name of the review.
- **Description.** A description of the review.
- **Start Date.** This will be used to determine recurring schedules as well.
- **Frequency.** You can set this to occur one time or to occur on a regular basis, such as monthly or annually.
- **Duration.** This determines how long each review should have to be completed.
- **End.** When the recurrence should end, if ever. You can choose **Never**, **End By**, or **Occurrences**. If you choose **Occurrences**, you can enter a number of times it should be run in the **Number Of Times** field.
- **Users.**
  - **Users To Review.** The users can either be group members or those assigned to an application.
  - **Scope.** The review can be open to guests only or everyone in the group.
- **Group.** Click the > icon to select a group.
- **Reviewers.** From the drop-down menu, you can select **Members For Self-Review**, **Selected Users**, or the **Group Owners**.
- **Programs.** You can choose the default program available; additional programs can be created by choosing **Identity Governance** > **Programs**.
- **Upon Completion Settings.**
  - **Auto Apply Results To Resource.** You can enable or disable the automatic application of review decisions.
  - **If Reviewers Don't Respond.** You can choose **No Change**, **Remove Access**, **Approve Access**, or **Take Recommendations**, which are auto-suggested actions based on user activity.
- **Advanced Settings.**
  - **Show Recommendations.** These recommendations are based on user activity.
  - **Require Reason On Approval.**
  - **Mail Notifications.** These notifications let people know they need to review a membership and notify admins when these reviews are complete.
  - **Reminders.**

FIGURE 1-4   A new access review being set up

Skill 1.3: Implement authentication methods

You have several tools with which to provide secure authentication options for your users. This skill will cover several of these tools, including multifactor authentication (MFA) with push notifications via the Authenticator app, as well as biometric authentication with Windows Hello.

This skill covers how to:

- Plan sign-in security
- Implement multifactor authentication (MFA)
- Manage and monitor MFA
- Plan and implement device authentication methods like Windows Hello
- Configure and manage Azure AD user authentication options

Plan sign-in security

With so many different methods of authentication and the ever-evolving landscape of cyber-security, Microsoft's Security Defaults feature helps simplify some basic security policies, which can be enabled by opening Azure AD and navigating to **Properties** > **Manage Security Defaults**. When you are done, the following policies will be activated:

- All users must register for Azure MFA.
- Admins must use MFA.
- Legacy authentication protocols are blocked.
- Users are required to perform MFA when necessary.
- Privileges such as access to the Azure portal have been restricted.

You can learn more about the specifics of each of these settings on the official documentation page for Security Defaults at *https://docs.microsoft.com/en-us/azure/active-directory/fundamentals/concept-fundamentals-security-defaults*.

> ***IMPORTANT*** **CONDITIONAL ACCESS VERSUS SECURITY DEFAULTS**
>
> If you plan on utilizing conditional access policies, as we cover in the next skill, you won't be able to benefit from Security Defaults, but you can set them up identically (and manually) as conditional access policies. The same documentation at *https://docs.microsoft.com/en-us/azure/active-directory/fundamentals/concept-fundamentals-security-defaults* has instructions on that process as well.

Aside from deciding if you want to utilize Security Defaults or custom conditional policies (possibly including policies matching all the security defaults anyway), your sign-in security strategy should consider questions such as:

- Should we have restrictions based on location?
- Do we require MFA for all or some users, and should it also be conditionally required?
- Should certain device characteristics be considered non-compliant?

In the following sections, we cover ways to respond to these questions and more.

Implement multifactor authentication (MFA)

Multifactor authentication (MFA) simply means we're asking users to provide an additional form of identification in order to sign in to access our organization's apps and data. Typically, MFA would involve your standard password combined with something like a biometric sign or a code sent to a separate device.

To enable MFA, you'll need an Azure AD Premium license. You can then use the Security Defaults mentioned in the last section or conditional access policies that require MFA as part of their execution. Conditional access policies are the recommended way of enforcing MFA.

Manage and monitor MFA

MFA sign-ins are reported like any other sign-in and are available in Azure AD's Sign-Ins report. To access this report, go to the Azure portal at *https://portal.azure.com* and select **Azure Active Directory** > **Users** > **Sign-Ins**.

On the Sign-Ins report, there's a **Conditional Access** column that shows whether a policy was triggered at the sign-in. You can select a sign-in event to see authentication details to find which policy was triggered, which MFA options were used, and the sign-in status (successful/failure).

Plan and implement device authentication methods like Windows Hello

Windows Hello for Business incorporates additional authentication methods such as biometrics (such as facial recognition or fingerprint) and device-specific pins and is exclusive to Windows 10 devices. In order to implement Windows Hello for SSO, devices must first be joined to Azure AD and Intune-enrolled.

Because planning and implementation will look differently for organizations based on their requirements and environment, Microsoft has a planning worksheet that can help determine Windows Hello planning needs. You can download this at *https://go.microsoft.com/fwlink/?linkid=852514* and follow the guide to complete it at *https://docs.microsoft.com/en-us/windows/security/identity-protection/hello-for-business/hello-planning-guide#planning-a-deployment*. See Figure 1-5 for the fields that appear on the blank worksheet.

For example, a completed worksheet for a cloud-only deployment of Windows Hello might include the following information:

- **Deployment**
    - **Deployment.** Cloud only
    - **Trust Type.** Key trust
    - **Device Registration.** Azure
    - **Key Registration.** Azure
    - **Directory Synchronization.** N/A
    - **Multifactor Authentication.** Azure MFA
- **Management**
    - **Domain Joined.** N/A
    - **Non-Domain Joined.** Modern management
- **Client**
    - **Domain Joined.** N/A
    - **Non-Domain Joined.** 1511 or later
- **Active Directory**
    - **Schema.** Windows Server 2016
    - **Domain Functional Level.** Windows Server 2008 R2 or later
    - **Forest Functional Level.** Windows Server 2008 R2 or later
    - **Domain Controller.** Windows Server 2016
- **Public Key Infrastructure**
    - **Certificate Authority.** N/A
    - **Registration Authority.** N/A
    - **Certificate Templates.** N/A
- **Cloud**
    - **Azure Account.** Yes
    - **Cloud Directory.** Yes
    - **Azure AD Premium.** Yes

Requirement		Data
1. Deployment		
Deployment	1a	
Trust Type	1b	
Device Registration	1c	
Key Registration	1d	
Directory Synchronization	1e	
Multifactor Authentication	1f	
2. Management		
Domain Joined	2a	
Non-Domain Joined	2b	
3. Client		
Domain Joined	3a	
Non-Domain Joined	3b	
4. Active Directory		
Schema	4a	**Windows Server 2016**
Domain Functional Level	4b	**Windows Server 2008 R2 or later**
Forest Functional Level	4c	**Windows Server 2008 R2 or later**
Domain Controller	4d	
5. Public Key Infrastructure		
Certificate Authority	5a	**Windows Server 2012 or later**
Registration Authority	5b	
Certificate Templates	5c	**Template Name** / **Issued To**
		Kerberos Authentication Certificate / **Domain Controllers**
6. Cloud		
Azure Account	6a	
Cloud Directory	6b	
Azure AD Premium	6c	

FIGURE 1-5 A blank Windows Hello for Business planning worksheet

Configure and manage Azure AD user authentication options

There are several ways a user can authenticate into Azure AD. The most common method is via a traditional username and password. Users could also download and use the Microsoft Authenticator App's passwordless sign-in; an OATH hardware token or FIDO2 security key; or an SMS-based passwordless sign-in.

In addition to these four primary options, users can have a secondary option to use when MFA is enabled. For example, after successfully passing authentication with a primary method, a user might then be prompted to use:

- OATH software tokens
- Voice call for code verification
- App passwords
- One of the unused primary methods as secondary (except for a traditional password)

For SSPR, users could also be prompted for:

- Security questions
- Email address, text message (SMS), or a voice call for code verification
- Microsoft Authenticator App approval

To enable passwordless authentication methods such as usage of the Microsoft Authenticator App, you must sign into the Azure portal at *https://portal.azure.com* and then select **Azure Active Directory** > **Security** > **Authentication Methods** > **Authentication Method Policy (Preview)**.

Now select either **FIDO2 Security Key**, **Microsoft Authenticator Passwordless Sign-In**, or **Text Message**. Each of the passwordless options has an **Enable/Disable** switch and can be enabled for all or specific users.

> *IMPORTANT* **MICROSOFT AUTHENTICATOR PASSWORDLESS SIGN-IN REQUIREMENT**
>
> Before you can enable this method so users can begin using Microsoft Authenticator, your tenant must be enabled for MFA with push notifications through the Authenticator app.

Skill 1.4: Implement conditional access

Conditional access allows you to specify conditions under which users and devices can access your organization's data in Office 365. In this skill, we'll cover the planning, configuration, and management of conditional access and compliance topics in Azure AD.

> **This skill covers how to:**
> - Plan for compliance and conditional access policies
> - Configure and manage device compliance for endpoint security
> - Implement and manage conditional access

Plan for compliance and conditional access policies

Conditional access policies can be configured in Azure AD (with a premium license) and Intune (with an Intune or Enterprise Mobility + Security license). The conditional access options from either location point to the same resource, but an Intune license adds mobile device and mobile application management options to what's included with just Azure AD, including device compliance policies.

Compliance policies are configured separately from conditional access policies, but they can be used within conditional access policies. For example, you can create a compliance policy for Intune-enrolled devices that states any Android device on a specific, older OS is out of compliance. Then, to prevent those unsupported devices from accessing company resources, you could create a conditional access policy like the one in Figure 1-6 that prevents access to non-compliant devices based on a device compliance policy.

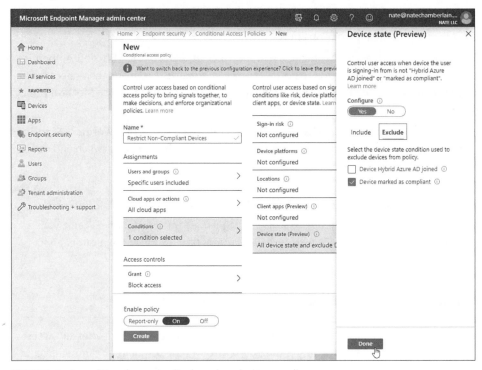

FIGURE 1-6   A conditional access policy based on device compliance

When planning for compliance and conditional access policies, you'll want to be thinking of questions such as:

- What characteristics determine compliant devices? (These could include OS version and build and mobile passcode requirements.)
- What policies exist in your organization that need to be incorporated into the compliance and conditional access policies somehow?
- What sign-in activity would be risky for users in your organization (such as foreign location sign-ins when users typically don't travel outside the country)?

Configure and manage device compliance for endpoint security

Access device compliance policies via the Microsoft Endpoint Manager admin center at *https:// endpoint.microsoft.com*. Once logged in, select **Devices** > **Compliance Policies** > **Create Policy** to create a new device compliance policy.

For each policy you create, you'll first select the Device platform for which the policy applies:

- Android device administrator
- Android Enterprise
- iOS/iPadOS
- macOS
- Windows 10 and later
- Windows 8.1 and later
- Windows Phone 8.1

You'll then name and describe the policy and configure compliance settings specific to that platform, such as:

- **Device Health.** BitLocker, Secure Boot, and whether code integrity is required
- **Device Properties.** Min and max OS versions and builds
- **Configuration Manager Compliance.** Compliant with Configuration Manager
- **System Security.** Mobile passwords, data encryption, firewall, antivirus, antimalware, and so on
- **Microsoft Defender ATP.** At or below a specific risk score

Next, you define what should happen if a device is considered noncompliant based on your compliance settings configuration. You have up to four different actions you can take at different times when a device is identified as noncompliant:

- **Mark Device Noncompliant**
- **Send Email To End User**
- **Remotely Lock The Noncompliant Device**
- **Retire The Noncompliant Device**

See Figure 1-7 for how these actions look when being configured in the policy creation wizard.

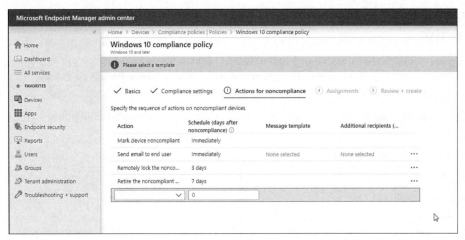

FIGURE 1-7 The Actions for noncompliance screen of a new compliance policy being configured

Next, you'll choose the security group(s) to which the policy applies and the group(s) that should be excluded from the policy.

The last step of the wizard is a review of everything you've configured in the policy. When you are satisfied, clicking **Create** completes the process.

Aside from compliance policies you create, you can also configure general compliance settings in the Microsoft Endpoint Manager admin center by choosing **Devices** > **Compliance Policies** > **Compliance Policy Settings**. These include:

- **Mark Devices With No Compliance Policy Assigned As.** Choose **Compliant** or **Not Compliant** to choose how to classify devices without an assigned compliance policy.
- **Enhanced Jailbreak Detection.** Use device's **Location Services** to have device check in with Intune more frequently.
- **Compliance Status Validity Period (Days).** Days without status report until a device is automatically considered noncompliant.

Also, you might have also noticed the **Message Template** option when creating a policy that includes the noncompliance action **Send Email To End User**. Message templates can be created via the **Notifications** node in the **Compliance Policies** section.

Another node to notice is the **Locations** node of the **Compliance Policies** section. This is where you can create locations that can be used in multiple compliance policies to determine device compliance (only for certain platforms).

> **REAL WORLD DEVICE COMPLIANCE**
>
> A common use for device compliance policies would be to require device passcodes to be used on personal devices being used to access company data and resources. This ensures that if a phone is lost, it's less likely to be picked up and used by someone other than its owner to access private company data.

Implement and manage conditional access

Conditional access policies are created in a similar fashion to how we configured the compliance policy in the previous section. Access conditional access policies via the Microsoft Endpoint Manager admin center at *https://endpoint.microsoft.com*. Once logged in, select **Endpoint Security** > **Conditional Access** > **New Policy** to create a new conditional access policy.

For each policy, you can configure the following:

- **Name.**
- **Assignments.**
    - **Users And Groups.** To whom the policy should apply, or who should be excluded.
    - **Cloud Apps Or Actions.**
        - **Cloud Apps.** Include or exclude **None**, **All**, or **Selected**.
        - **User Actions.** Register security information.
    - **Conditions.** Identify which criteria the policy will allow or deny access?
        - **Sign-In Risk**
        - **Device Platforms**
        - **Locations**
        - **Client apps**
        - **Device state**
- **Access Controls**
    - **Grant. Grant Access** or **Block Access** and set the granted requirements.
    - **Session.** Conditional access app control, sign-in frequency time period, and persistent browser sessions.

Figure 1-8 shows a simple conditional access policy that applies to all cloud apps for selected users/groups. It's a common policy that is just requiring MFA to access the cloud apps.

Lastly, you can choose to enable the policy or leave it off for now. The default option is **Report-Only**, which is good for testing the effect the policy will have on users and for glimpsing the actual scope of its configuration compared to your expectations.

One scenario you might run across when working with conditional access policies is the need to restrict access to VPN connectivity for non-compliant devices. This works similarly to what we've covered—combining a compliance policy with a conditional access policy—but you'll also create a VPN certificate in the Azure portal and deploy it to your VPN server. In your conditional access policy, your cloud app would then be VPN server. See a full write-up on this process at *https://docs.microsoft.com/en-us/windows-server/remote/remote-access/vpn/ad-ca-vpn-connectivity-windows10*.

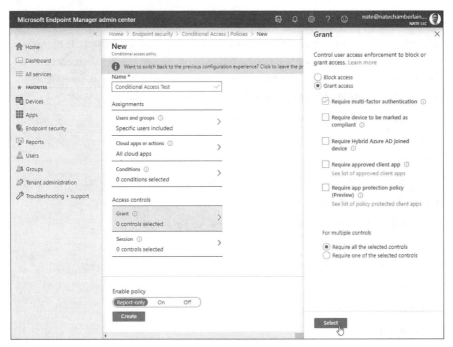

FIGURE 1-8 The Grant pane of access controls showing what can be required of users who are attempting to access

Skill 1.5: Implement role-based access control (RBAC)

Azure role-based access control (RBAC) allows you the ability to divide responsibility by role for and access to management of various machines, networks, resource groups, and so on. These roles and their assignments will be covered in this skill.

> **This skill covers how to:**
> - Plan for roles
> - Configure roles
> - Audit roles

Plan for roles

RBAC roles can be Allow or Deny assignments and are additive in nature, meaning that multiple allow assignments result in the sum of their allowances for the user they're applied to. A Deny assignment overrides any Allow assignments and can remove access to certain areas for specific users as well.

Each assignment consists of three components:

- **Security principal.** Object requesting access.
  - **User.** Azure AD user.
  - **Group.** Azure AD group.
  - **Service principal.** Security identity for specific resource access.
  - **Managed identity.** Auto-managed identity in Azure AD.
- **Role definition.** Also known as a "role" and encompasses all its specific permissions.
  - **Scope.** Resources to which the assignment applies.

Scopes are structured hierarchically, meaning a role assigned to a parent level applies to its children as well. The scope resource hierarchy is as follows:

- Management group
  - Subscription
    - Resource group
      - Resource

Configure roles

Role assignments can be created in the Azure portal (*https://portal.azure.com*). Once in the portal, click **Subscriptions**, select a subscription for which you'll make RBAC assignments, and then select **Access Control (IAM)**, as shown in Figure 1-9.

FIGURE 1-9 Access control (IAM) link in the Azure Portal Subscription details screen

From Access control (IAM), you can:

- Add a role assignment (Owner, Contributor, Reader, and dozens of specific roles)
- View role assignments

- View deny assignments
- Create a custom role (when one of the many default options doesn't quite fit)

You can also use PowerShell to assign roles, using the *New-AzRoleAssignment* cmdlet, and remove them with the *Remove-AzRoleAssignment* cmdlet. Specifically, for assigning at the resource group scope level (second-lowest level of scope hierarchy), you'd also need to declare *-SignInName*, *-RoleDefinitionName*, and *-ResourceGroupName* properties, as shown in this example:

```
New-AzRoleAssignment -SignInName nate@natechamberlain.com -RoleDefinitionName "Virtual
    Machine Contributor" -ResourceGroupName comp-sales
```

You can find additional documentation on using PowerShell for RBAC assignments at *https:// docs.microsoft.com/en-us/azure/role-based-access-control/role-assignments-powershell*.

Audit roles

The Azure **Activity Log**, located on the details screen for a subscription right above **Access Control (IAM)**, lets you easily audit role configuration changes in that subscription's RBAC including:

- New assignments
- Deleted assignments
- Created or modified custom roles
- Deleted custom roles

You can also access the Activity Log by searching for it in the Azure portal and then filtering to the subscription(s) for which you're interested in auditing RBAC.

The results can be exported to a CSV file.

Skill 1.6: Implement Azure AD Privileged Identity Management (PIM)

Privileged Identity Management (PIM) enables your organization to protect important resources across Azure, Azure AD, Intune, and Office 365 apps and services by managing and auditing access to them. This skill covers the planning and implementation of PIM in an environment.

> **This skill covers how to:**
> - Plan for Azure PIM
> - Implement and configure Azure PIM roles
> - Manage Azure PIM role assignments

Plan for Azure PIM

PIM enhances the security of an organization by allowing for features such as just-in-time (JIT) access requests for temporary role elevation, requiring of approvals and MFA for elevation, and audit PIM activities at a detail appropriate for rigorous audit needs. In order to use PIM, you must have an Azure AD Premium P2, Microsoft 365 M5, or Enterprise Mobility + Security (EMS) E5 license.

When planning for PIM, you should consider things such as:

- Should granting privileged roles be subject to approval?
- How could JIT access requests improve current practices?
- Which roles should be re-evaluated and possibly put under an access review?

Implement and configure Azure PIM roles

Once you're properly licensed to begin using PIM, you can configure Azure AD and Azure roles to begin using it. Start by going to the Azure portal and searching for **Azure AD Privileged Identity Management**; click the result once it appears and then select **Azure AD Roles** > **Settings**.

Next, select a role for which you'll modify role settings. In Figure 1-10, you can see settings for the Teams Service Administrator role as an example. These settings, such as how long a role can be activated for, are an important part of your governance strategy.

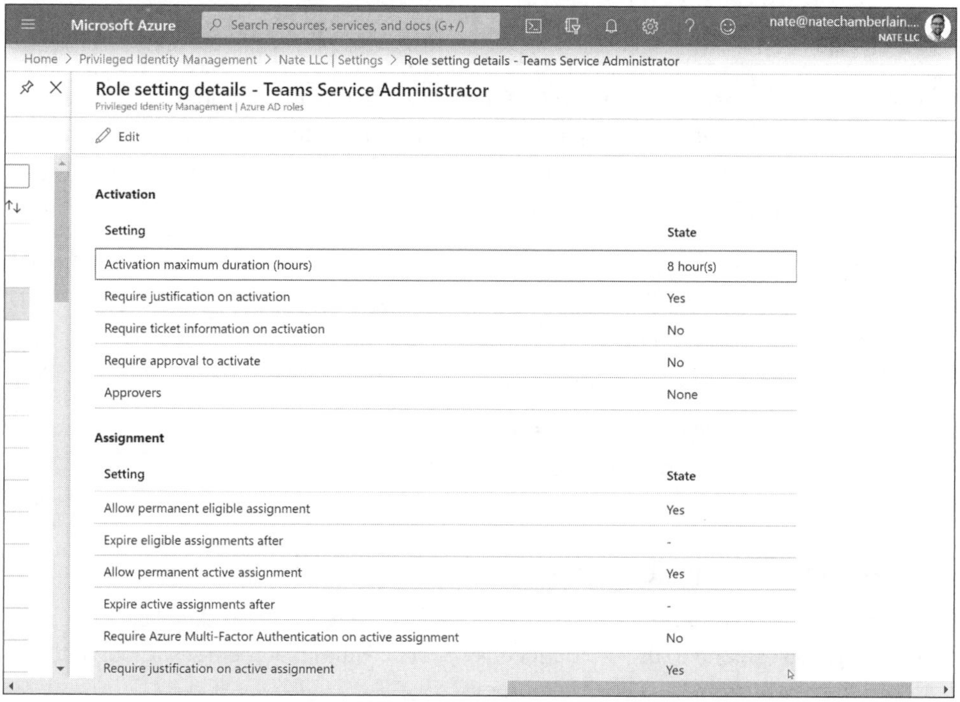

FIGURE 1-10   Azure PIM role settings for the Teams Service Administrator role

The distinction between assigning roles in Azure AD versus PIM is that with PIM, you can still assign permanent admin roles but gain the additional ability to make somebody *eligible* for a role that they can request activation of in a JIT scenario.

To assign someone as eligible for a role, you'd select the **Assignments** node in the PIM screen, click **Add Assignments**, and select the role and member(s) to whom you're assigning it. Then choose whether they're **Eligible** or **Active** and whether that status is **Permanent** or **Temporary** (for dates you would provide).

Manage Azure PIM role assignments

To manage existing assignments, you can use the **Assignments** node of PIM to search for members and see their roles separated in tabs for **Eligible Roles**, **Active Roles**, and **Expired Roles**, just as you could for your own on the **My Roles** node.

For each role listed, you can **Remove**, **Update**, or **Extend** the assignment.

If you are an approver and have requests for activation or extension, you can work through those in the **Approve Requests** node.

Lastly, if your organization has implemented Access Reviews, those can be created and monitored on the **Access Reviews** menu node. These are created much in the same way as normal Access Reviews, such as for O365 group membership; however, target privileged roles as opposed to groups. They can still be assigned to the role assignee or someone else.

Skill 1.7: Implement Azure AD Identity Protection

Azure AD Identity Protection is an Azure AD Premium P2 feature that includes user risk and sign-in risk policies and alerts that help you stay on top of mitigating the potential of data loss risk. This skill will go over the implementation of both policy types, configuration of Identity Protection alerts, and managing risk events.

> **This skill covers how to:**
> - Implement user risk policy
> - Implement sign-in risk policy
> - Configure Identity Protection alerts
> - Review and respond to risk events

Implement user risk policy

The first of two available Identity Protection policies we cover is the user risk policy. This policy helps identify and respond to user account behavior or activities that seem suspicious and indicate the account might have been compromised.

The policy will catch detections of the following types:

- Leaked credentials (checked against the known leaks database)
- Azure AD threat intelligence (atypical behavior or consistent with known attack patterns)

To access and implement the User Risk Policy, navigate to the Azure portal and then click **Azure Active Directory** > **Security** > **Identity Protection** > **User Risk Policy**.

To set up the policy, you'll need to make decisions for each of the following:

- **Assignments**
  - **Users.** (Include or exclude all users or specific users and groups)
  - **Conditions (User Risk Threshold)**
- **Controls**
  - **Access. Allow** or **Block** with an option to **Require Password Reset** if allowed

> **NOTE   USER RISK THRESHOLD CONDITION**
>
> Microsoft recommends setting the **User Risk Threshold** to **High**.

If users are flagged for risk, we can enable self-remediation of risk flags as long as users are registered for SSPR.

Implement sign-in risk policy

The second policy is the sign-in risk policy. This policy helps identify and respond to risky or unusual account sign-in behavior that might indicate the account has been compromised.

The policy will catch detections of the following types:

- Anonymous IP address
- Atypical travel
- Malware-linked IP address
- Unfamiliar sign-in properties
- Admin-confirmed user compromised
- Malicious IP address
- Suspicious inbox manipulation rules
- Impossible travel

To access and implement the sign-in risk policy, navigate to the Azure portal and then click **Azure Active Directory** > **Security** > **Identity Protection** > **Sign-In Risk Policy**.

To set up the policy, you'll need to make decisions for each of the following:

- **Assignments**
  - **Users.** Include or exclude all users or specific users and groups
  - **Conditions. Sign-In Risk** level
- **Controls**
  - **Access. Allow** or **Block** with the option to **Require Password Reset** if allowed

> **NOTE SIGN-IN RISK THRESHOLD CONDITION**
> Microsoft recommends setting the **Sign-In Risk Threshold** to **Medium And Above.**

If users are flagged for risk, we can enable self-remediation of risk flags as long as users are registered for Azure MFA.

Configure Identity Protection alerts

Configuring alerts in Azure Identity Protection involves just a few steps. First, you'll navigate to alerts via the Azure portal and then click **Azure Active Directory** > **Security** > **Identity Protection** > **Users At Risk Detected Alerts**.

For the alert, you can choose:

- Risk level on which to alert (**Low**, **Medium**, or **High**)
- Which users are notified
- Additional emails to include on alerts (recipient must have Azure Identity Protection portal access)

Review and respond to risk events

Risk events are separated into risky users, risky sign-ins, and risk detections in Azure AD Identity Protection. To access these reports, you can go to the Azure portal and then select **Azure Active Directory** > **Security** > **Identity Protection** and look along the left-hand navigation for the three nodes under **Report**.

For each risky user who appears, you can:

- Investigate that user's sign-ins and risk detections
- View specific information about each event
- Reset password
- Confirm user compromised
- Dismiss user risk
- Block user
- Investigate with Azure ATP (if licensed)

Thought Experiments

In the following Thought Experiments, apply what you've learned in this chapter. You can find answers to these questions in the "Thought Experiment Answers" section at the end of this chapter.

Secure Microsoft 365 hybrid environments

1. You receive an Unhealthy identity synchronization error notification via email. Which of the following is a potential cause?

   A. Demo/trial license for Azure AD expired

   B. Duplicate users found in sync

   C. Password hash synchronization not enabled

   D. Password writeback not enabled

2. Azure AD Connect sync was installed using Express settings, or the default authentication settings. Password hash synchronization will be disabled by default.

   A. True

   B. False

3. Which authentication method must be enabled to utilize premium Azure AD features like Identity Protection?

   A. Password hash synchronization (PHS)

   B. Pass-through authentication (PTA)

   C. Federation (AD FS)

Secure identities

1. Self-service password reset can be configured for one or multiple security groups.

   A. True

   B. False

2. To create an Accounting group that has automatic membership in Azure AD, you must select _____ for membership type, then set Property to _____ and Value to equals _____.

   A. Assigned | Group | Accounting

   B. Dynamic user | Group | Accounting

   C. Dynamic user | Department | Accounting

   D. Assigned | Department | Accounting

3. The owner of the Pride Month Committee group is the current chair of the committee. They're about to welcome the incoming chair and would like that incoming chair to review the membership of their Azure AD group during their first month. What solution would be appropriate to configure?

   A. Add the new chair to the security group allowed to use self-service password reset

   B. Create a new Azure AD group of Office 365 type with the new chair as owner

   C. Assign the incoming chair a new one-time access review beginning their first day

   D. Assign the existing chair an annual access review beginning their last day

Implement authentication methods

1. You need to make sure users connecting to the company's O365 environment while outside the main office are required to use MFA. What will you create to ensure this?

   A. A compliance policy

   B. A user risk policy

   C. A sign-in risk policy

   D. A conditional access policy

2. Your office has four branches. Their IP addresses and ranges are as follows:

   - New York: 192.0.2.0/24

   - San Francisco: 192.168.0.0/16

   - Miami: 198.51.100.0/24

   - Kansas City: 203.0.113.0/24

   How would you go about creating an MFA policy that doesn't require Kansas City users to use MFA when connecting from IP addresses in their range, but requires everyone else to do so?

   A. Add 198.51.100.0/24 as a trusted IP and include it in the policy requiring MFA

   B. Add 203.0.113.0/24 as a trusted IP and exclude it in the policy requiring MFA

   C. Add all IPs as trusted IPs and include them in the policy requiring MFA

   D. Add all IPs as trusted IPs and exclude them in the policy requiring MFA

3. Would the policy shown in Figure 1-11 enforce MFA for the specific users it includes, assuming the conditions are met?

   A. Yes, MFA will be enforced upon clicking Create.

   B. No, MFA will not be enforced upon clicking Create.

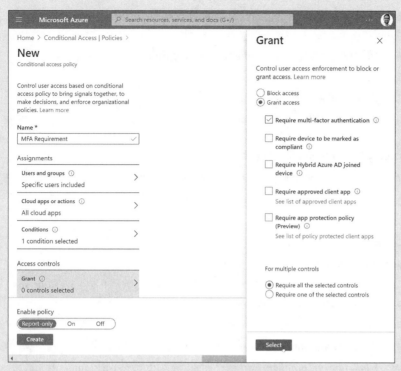

FIGURE 1-11 New conditional access policy's Access controls configuration blade

Implement conditional access

1. In order to prevent access to users signing in from noncompliant devices, you must first have configured what?

   A. A named location in Azure AD

   B. Multifactor authentication (MFA)

   C. Identity Protection alerts

   D. A compliance policy

2. What should you create in order to restrict users from accessing company resources when they're not connecting from the main office network? Select all that could work.

   A. A trusted IP and a compliance policy

   B. A named location and a conditional access policy

   C. A trusted IP and a conditional access policy

   D. A named location and a compliance policy

3. Before users' access to company data via VPN can be restricted, what must first be done?

   A. Add VPN server as a cloud app in your conditional access policy

   B. Deploy a certificate to your VPN server

   C. Download a certificate from Azure AD

   D. Create a certificate in Azure AD

Implement role-based access control (RBAC)

1. Which of the following is not an RBAC security principal?

   A. User

   B. Group

   C. Managed Identity

   D. Subscription

2. A user has both an allow and deny assignment in RBAC. Which one overrides the other if they conflict on a particular allowance?

   A. The allow assignment overrides

   B. The deny assignment overrides

3. Which PowerShell command is used to make new RBAC role assignments for a user?

   A. *New-AzRoleAssignment*

   B. *Assign-AzRoleAssignment*

   C. *New-RBACRoleAssignment*

   D. *Apply-RBACRoleAssignment*

Implement Azure AD Privileged Identity Management

1. Your CIO requests that anybody given the Exchange administrator role has a maximum assignment to that role of 30 days before they must request an extension or the role expires until requested for activation again. Which solution can you use here (assuming an EMS E5 license)?

   A. Azure AD Identity Protection

   B. Azure AD Privileged Identity Management

   C. Azure AD Audit Logs

   D. Azure AD Role Administration Center

2. You need to make it easy for people to get temporary access to admin capabilities without assigning them a permanent active role. What should you do to accomplish this?

   A. Make the user active for a role for a specific time period

   B. Make the user eligible for a role

   C. Review your activation requests

   D. Initiate a round of access reviews

3. Which node of PIM allows you to extend role assignments for users?

   A. Access reviews

   B. My roles

   C. Approve requests

   D. Assignments

Implement Azure AD Identity Protection

1. A manager asks to be included on Identity Protection email alerts that go out for high-risk events. What do you need to do first?

   A. Make sure the manager is licensed to access Azure AD Identity Protection

   B. Add the manager's email address as an additional recipient for high-risk alerts

2. You want to automatically respond to risky sign-ins by still allowing the sign-in activity but requiring MFA as part of it. Does the Sign-In Risk policy snippet shown in Figure 1-12 achieve this goal?

   A. Yes

   B. No

FIGURE 1-12 Sign-In Risk Access setting set to Allow Access and Require Multi-Factor Authentication

3. Which Azure AD Identity Protection policy allows for requiring a user to change his or her password once identified as a risky user?

   A. User Risk Policy

   B. Sign-In Risk Policy

   C. Conditional Access Policy

   D. Compliance Policy

Thought Experiment Answers

Following are answers to the questions posed in the "Thought Experiments" section of this chapter.

Secure Microsoft 365 hybrid environments

1. A
2. B
3. A

Secure identities

1. B
2. C
3. C

Implement authentication methods

1. D
2. B
3. B

Implement conditional access

1. D
2. B and C
3. D

Implement role-based access control (RBAC)

1. D
2. B
3. A

Implement Azure AD Privileged Identity Management

1. B
2. B
3. D

Implement Azure AD Identity Protection

1. A
2. A
3. A

CHAPTER 2

Implement and manage threat protection

This chapter is all about Microsoft Threat Protection and includes five objectives. They address how to protect a hybrid organization, how to protect devices, how to protect applications, and how to protect the SaaS applications and data within Office 365.

Skills in this chapter:

- Skill 2.1: Implement an enterprise hybrid threat protection solution
- Skill 2.2: Implement device threat protection
- Skill 2.3: Implement and manage device and application protection
- Skill 2.4: Implement and manage Office 365 ATP
- Skill 2.5: Implement Azure Sentinel for Microsoft 365

Skill 2.1: Implement an enterprise hybrid threat protection solution

Enterprise hybrid threat protection is about addressing the challenges facing an organization with applications and identities that are served from both on-premises infrastructure and cloud solutions, such as Office 365. Identity is the new security boundary, and the goals of this objective are detecting when attempts are made to compromise identities, as well as ensuring authenticated users are not abusing their access.

This skill covers how to:

- Planning an Azure Advanced Threat Protection (ATP) solution
- Install and configure Azure ATP
- Manage Azure ATP Workspace Health
- Generate Azure ATP reports
- Integrate Azure ATP with Microsoft Defender ATP
- Manage suspicious activities

Planning an Azure Advanced Threat Protection (ATP) solution

Azure ATP requires some pre-work in order to successfully deploy, including ensuring that your domain controllers meet the hardware requirements, have the necessary software prerequisites installed, and have the required connectivity to Azure ATP endpoints in the cloud.

Capacity planning

You need to download and run the Azure ATP Sizing tool, TriSizingTool.exe, from Microsoft and run it from a workstation or server that can connect to all domain controllers in your environment. Doing so will evaluate the CPU utilization, available RAM, and network I/O, and it will make recommendations where more hardware needs to be added to domain controllers that are to run the Azure ATP agent.

The minimum hardware recommendations include:

- **CPU.** At least two cores.
- **RAM.** At least 6GB.
- **Disk space.** A minimum of 5GB free and at least 10GB free is recommended.

Those are really the bare minimums, and if your Active Directory has a larger number of objects, you should expect to need more. For the best performance, your domain controllers should have enough RAM to cache the entire NTDS.DIT in memory on top of the operating system requirements and any other software running on the domain controllers, so it is common for the Azure ATP Sizing tool to recommend more RAM.

If you cannot run the Azure ATP Sizing tool, there is a manual method you can use to estimate hardware needs, which is documented at *https://docs.microsoft.com/en-us/azure-advanced-threat-protection/atp-capacity-planning#manual-sizing*, but you really should use the tool to automate this process.

> ***REAL WORLD*** **VIRTUALIZED DOMAIN CONTROLLERS AND MEMORY**
>
> It's common to find domain controllers running as guests of a hypervisor host and with dynamically allocated memory. If that is the case in your environment, expect the sizing tool to report that these domain controllers will all need additional RAM. While it's always recommended that domain controllers be provisioned with a fixed RAM assignment, it is a requirement when running Azure ATP. Allocate a fixed amount of RAM or deploy the standalone agent, which also requires a fixed allocation of RAM. You may choose to try running with less RAM than the sizing tool calls for and increase the allocation of memory until you find what works in your environment. Just keep in mind that if there is not enough RAM on the domain controller, you may miss events. This means you should try to quickly dial in to what works for you.

If the tool identifies domain controllers that require more resources than you have available to allocate, you can consider deploying Azure ATP using the Azure ATP Standalone deployment. With this approach, you deploy one or more additional servers that will run the Azure

ATP Standalone agent and you mirror (span) the network switch port for your domain control-lers to a monitor interface on the Azure ATP Standalone server. One Azure ATP Standalone server can monitor multiple domain controllers in this way, as long as network traffic from all the domain controllers does not exceed the capacity of the Standalone server, which is estimated at 100,000 packets per second. This out-of-band deployment makes it harder for an attacker to determine that they are being watched, but it comes with the additional costs of deploying more servers.

EXAM TIP

Deploying the Azure ATP Standalone sensor has pros and cons. The pros include not need-ing to deploy additional software to domain controllers to upgrade their hardware and that the out-of-band deployment can make it harder for an adversary to detect. The cons include the additional cost, the need for a mirror port, and that you lose the ability to directly capture ETW events on the domain controller, which are necessary for certain detections, in-cluding LDAP-based reconnaissance. You can get around this by configuring event forward-ing from domain controllers to the standalone sensor, but that does increase the complexity of your deployment.

Prerequisites

The Azure ATP agent can be installed on domain controllers, including RODCs, running the following operating systems:

- Server 2008 R2 SP1 (not including Server Core)
- Windows Server 2012
- Windows Server 2012 R2
- Windows Server 2016 (including Windows Server Core but not Windows Nano Server)
- Windows Server 2019 (including Windows Core but not Windows Nano Server)

Server 2019 requires that KB4487044 be installed. In all cases, .Net Framework 4.7 will be installed if it is not already present and might require a reboot.

The Azure ATP standalone agent can be installed on servers running the following operat-ing systems:

- Windows Server 2012 R2
- Windows Server 2016 (including Server Core) single standalone agent can be used to monitor multiple domain controllers, assuming that there is sufficient hardware, and the network switch supports mirroring traffic from multiple ports and can be used to moni-tor domains with a functional level of 2003 or later. The server running the standalone agent can be domain-joined or it can run in workgroup mode. If it is in workgroup mode, ensure that time synchronization is set up with the domain(s) to monitor.

It should have at least two network interface cards. One will be used for management, while the other will be connected to the span port, so it can monitor network traffic for the domain controller(s).

You also need to ensure that all domain controllers or standalone agents that you will deploy have Internet connectivity to the appropriate Azure endpoints. If you are using a proxy server or other web filtering solution, permit connectivity to the endpoints documented at *https://docs.microsoft.com/en-us/azure-advanced-threat-protection/configure-proxy*.

See Table 2-1 for an overview of the required endpoints.

TABLE 2-1 Azure ATP service endpoints

Service Location	*.atp.azure.com DNS Record
US	*triprd1wcusw1sensorapi.atp.azure.com* *triprd1wcuswb1sensorapi.atp.azure.com* *triprd1wcuse1sensorapi.atp.azure.com*
Europe	*triprd1wceun1sensorapi.atp.azure.com* *triprd1wceuw1sensorapi.atp.azure.com*
Asia	*triprd1wcasse1sensorapi.atp.azure.com*

Install and configure Azure ATP

Installing and configuring Azure ATP involves connecting to the portal, providing information for your set up, downloading the installation package, and deploying it to the servers.

The Azure ATP portal

When you sign in to the portal for the first time, you will create the instance of Azure ATP for your environment. You will be prompted for the username (NetBIOS format), password, and Active Directory domain name for the service account you will use; this account should be a user account with Read-Only access to your environment. Once you enter the information, you can download the sensor setup file. This zip file will install either the Azure ATP agent on a do-main controller or the Azure ATP Standalone agent on a non-domain controller, and it contains the installer and a configuration file. You will also have to copy the Access key, which is used to establish the initial connection to your Azure ATP instance. Once installed, all authentication is through certificates.

Azure ATP supports RBAC through three built-in security groups. To access the Azure ATP console, a user must be a member of at least one of these groups. At the time of this writing, custom RBAC is not available. The built-in roles are listed in Table 2-2.

TABLE 2-2 Azure ATP roles and capabilities

Capability	Azure ATP Administrators	Azure ATP Users	Azure ATP Viewers
Log in to the portal	Yes	Yes	Yes
Modify security alert status	Yes	Yes	No
Export security alerts	Yes	Yes	Yes
Download reports	Yes	Yes	Yes

Modify monitoring alert status	Yes	No	No
Modify Azure ATP configuration	Yes	No	No
Modify data sources	Yes	No	No
Modify updates	Yes	No	No
Modify scheduled reports	Yes	Yes	No
Modify tags	Yes	Yes	No
Modify exclusions	Yes	Yes	No
Modify language	Yes	Yes	No
Modify notifications	Yes	Yes	No
Modify detections	Yes	Yes	No
View profiles and alerts	Yes	Yes	Yes

Membership in the Azure ATP RBAC groups is managed through the Groups Management blade in the Azure Active Directory portal, as shown in Figure 2-1.

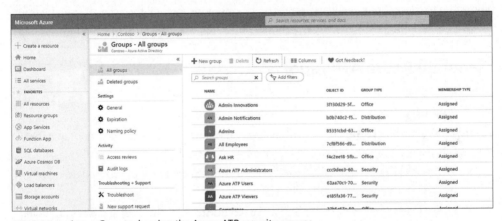

FIGURE 2-1 Azure Groups showing the Azure ATP security groups

EXAM TIP

Any user who is a Global Administrator or a Security Administrator is automatically an Azure ATP Administrator.

Manage Azure ATP Workspace Health

The Azure ATP portal includes a section on Workspace Health, where issues such as connectivity, disconnected sensors, or service account authentication are reported. The Health icon shown in Figure 2-2 will indicate whether there is any detected problem by displaying a red dot over the icon.

FIGURE 2-2 The Azure Advanced Threat Protection menu indicating a problem with Workspace Health

To access Workspace Health and view the issue, simply click the icon. Workspace Health will list the problem or problems detected and provide information on how to correct the issue. It's important to check this to see if an agent is no longer reporting or if the account used by the service can no longer authenticate; you should remediate any problems immediately.

Generate Azure ATP reports

The Reports page in the Azure ATP portal lets you download four report types:

- **Summary.** This is a summary of alerts and health issues.
- **Modifications To Sensitive Groups.** Every modification to sensitive groups in Active Directory, including modifications that generated an alert.
- **Passwords Exposed In Cleartext.** All LDAP authentications that exposed user passwords in cleartext.
- **Lateral Movements Paths To Sensitive Accounts.** Sensitive accounts at risk of being compromised through lateral movement techniques.

By default, the report will show the last seven days' data, but you can use the calendar selector to configure a custom date range. Reports are downloaded as Excel files. You can also schedule any of the reports on a Daily, Weekly, or Monthly basis and at a specific time, as shown in Figure 2-3.

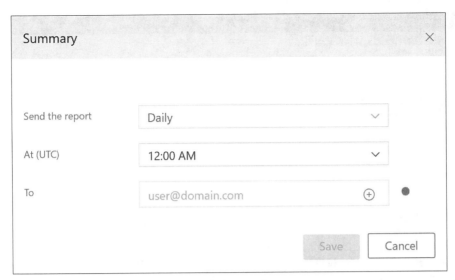

FIGURE 2-3 Scheduling Azure ATP reports in the portal

Integrate Azure ATP with Microsoft Defender ATP

Azure ATP can integrate with Microsoft Defender ATP, integrating the UEBA capabilities on domain controllers with EDR capabilities on endpoints to enhance the protections provided by both. To enable this integration, you must do so in both the Azure ATP portal, and the Microsoft Defender ATP Security Center.

In the Azure ATP portal, under **Configuration**, simply switch the **Integration With Windows Defender ATP** slider to **On** and select **Save**, as shown in Figure 2-4.

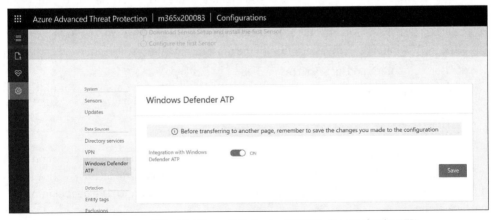

FIGURE 2-4 Integrating Azure ATP with Microsoft Defender ATP (Windows Defender ATP)

Next, access Microsoft Defender ATP at *https://securitycenter.windows.com*, and under **Settings** > **Advanced Features**, enable **Azure ATP Integration** (see Figure 2-5) and click **Save Preferences**.

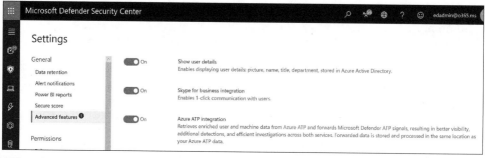

FIGURE 2-5 Integrating Microsoft Defender ATP with Azure ATP

MORE INFO

If you're paying attention, you noticed that Figure 2-4 shows integration between Azure ATP and Microsoft Defender ATP shows "Windows Defender ATP." Microsoft renamed Windows Defender ATP to Microsoft Defender ATP with the introduction of first-party support for Mac OSX and the upcoming support for Linux. It takes time to update all the places it's called Windows Defender ATP, and at the time of this writing, the Azure ATP portal still shows the old name. By the time you're reading this, it will no doubt show the proper name, Microsoft Defender ATP.

Once enabled, if there is a detection in Azure ATP that involves an entity in Microsoft Defender ATP, an icon will appear in the profile for any detection in Azure ATP that will take you to the corresponding information in Microsoft Defender ATP.

Manage suspicious activities

Managing suspicious activities requires that you monitor Azure ATP and review alerts, either in the portal or in the summary emails. When you log in to the Azure ATP portal, you will automatically be taken to the Security Alerts Timeline if there are any Security Alerts. There, you will see alerts in chronological order, starting with the most recent. Alerts will include:

- User, computers, and/or resources involved
- The time of the activity
- Severity
- Status

You can hover your mouse pointer over the alert to surface the mini profile (integration with Microsoft Defender ATP is very valuable here), and you can share the security alert with others through email or download the alert. You can also click the alert to dive deeper into the timeline of the event.

Alerts are categorized as follows, which aligns with the phases in an attack-kill chain:

- Reconnaissance
- Compromised credentials

- Lateral movement
- Domain dominance
- Data exfiltration

By default, preview detections are enabled so that you can see the newest insights. You can disable this in the **Configuration** blade, but it's a good idea to keep these enabled so you are aware of things going on in the environment, even if they are not considered mainstream detections yet.

You can filter security alerts based on **Status**—**All**, **Open**, **Closed**, or **Suppressed**—and by **Severity**; your choices are **High**, **Medium**, and **Low**. You can choose **Suppress Alerts** or **Exclude Entities From Raising Alerts** if you need to reduce the noise from events that, in your specific case, are normal or allowed. For example, you might want to suppress alerts regarding a legacy application that must use LDAP authentication or suppress an administrator who runs a security scanning application against multiple machines. Also, you can delete events.

> **IMPORTANT**
>
> While only Azure ATP Administrators can perform these actions, they really shouldn't perform a delete. Deleting alerts is permanent, and they cannot be restored. Make sure you have long-term storage for alerts; otherwise, you should close alerts instead of deleting them.

Skill 2.2: Implement device threat protection

Endpoints include workstations, servers, laptops, and mobile devices, and they are what your users use to interact with your applications and data every day. Protecting these endpoints is critical to the overall security of your organization, and technologies to help with this include Endpoint Protection, Endpoint Detection and Response, and Threat and Vulnerability Management. In this skill, we will cover Microsoft Defender Advanced Threat Protection and how it is a key component of Microsoft Threat Protection.

> **IMPORTANT**
>
> In early 2019, Microsoft renamed Windows Defender Advanced Threat Protection as Microsoft Defender Advanced Threat Protection; Microsoft made the change largely because it announced that the product would soon include a first-party client for non-Windows platforms. At the time of this writing, the Mac client is generally available, but there are still many Microsoft and other web pages and documentation that use the older name. While Microsoft is working on updating all documentation and consoles to use the new Microsoft Defender ATP name, blog posts and screenshots might still show the older name. Don't let that throw you.

Plan and implement a Microsoft Defender ATP solution

Planning and implementing Microsoft Defender ATP is straightforward. You need to be aware of the licensing requirements, the supported operating systems, and the deployment methods available to you. Microsoft Defender ATP is licensed as a part of the Microsoft 365 E5 suite and is also available with Windows Enterprise E5 (and the educational versions of those licenses). Hardware requirements are the same as for the operating systems. Remember, Microsoft Defender ATP is already a part of the Windows 10, Windows Server 2019, and Windows Server 2016 1803 operating systems. Supported operating systems at the time of this writing include:

■ Windows 7 SP1 Enterprise

■ Windows 7 SP1 Pro

■ Windows 8.1 Enterprise

■ Windows 8.1 Pro

■ Windows 10, version 1607 or later

■ Windows Server 2008 R2 SP1

■ Windows Server 2012 R2

■ Windows Server 2016

■ Windows Server 2016, version 1803

■ Windows Server 2019

■ macOS Mojave, macOS High Sierra, and macOS Sierra

> **IMPORTANT**
>
> While you can protect servers using Microsoft Defender ATP, the licenses included in Microsoft 365 E5 and Windows E5 only cover the Windows workstation products. To protect servers, you must onboard them to the Azure Security Center, which charges based on a consumption model.

When initially configuring Microsoft Defender ATP, you will choose the location where your data will be stored, which at the time of this writing, includes the United States, the United Kingdom, and the European Union. Once selected, you cannot change this; if you later change your mind, you must tear down and start over again. You will also choose how long data will be stored, with options from 30 to 180 days.

Deployment methods include locally run script, Group Policy Object, SCCM, and Intune, as well as other third-party MDM and software-deployment solutions, as shown in Figure 2-6.

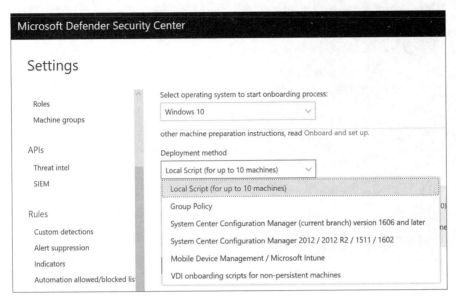

FIGURE 2-6 Microsoft Defender ATP deployment methods

For Windows 10 and Server 2019, deployment is really nothing more than pushing the configuration that specifies the Microsoft Defender ATP tenant and API key used to establish the initial connection. For older operating systems, deployment includes the installation of the Microsoft Defender ATP agent by way of an MSI file. For non-persistent VDI, note that only Windows 10 is supported.

Note that both the Windows diagnostic data service and Windows Defender Antivirus are enabled. If either of these services are disabled, Microsoft Defender ATP onboarding will fail. If you are using a third-party antivirus solution, Windows Defender Antivirus must still be enabled, though it will run in passive mode, and you will want to make sure that the Windows Defender Antivirus Early Launch Antimalware (ELAM) driver is enabled.

Manage Microsoft Defender ATP

Managing Microsoft Defender ATP is as simple as using a supported web browser and being either a Global Administrator or a Security Administrator. Additional RBAC can be configured once Microsoft Defender ATP is initially set up. You can create roles with varied capabilities and assign permissions as appropriate to your organization's needs (see Figure 2-7).

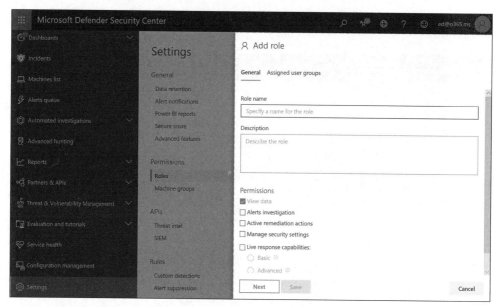

FIGURE 2-7 Adding a role in Microsoft Defender ATP

You should be familiar with each of the areas in the Microsoft Defender ATP console and what you would use each one to do.

Dashboards

Dashboards include information you would want to see first or even to keep on display in a security operations center (SOC). All offer high-level insights, and you can drill down to get more details. The dashboards include Security Operations, Secure Score, and Threat analytics.

Incidents

Anything that Microsoft Defender ATP detects is tracked as an incident. The Incidents area allows you to view and work with incidents. You can filter, classify, and assign incidents and see details. Full details are available in the **Alerts** associated with the incident (see Figure 2-8).

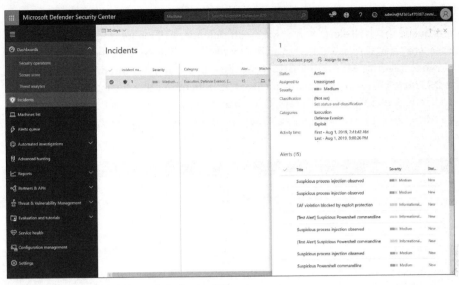

FIGURE 2-8 Incidents in Microsoft Defender ATP

Machines list

The Machines list panel displays all the enrolled machines in Microsoft Defender ATP, enables you to find or filter for a specific machine or version, and allows you to see all details of the machine, including the last logged on user; the IP address of the system; active alerts and incidents; the exposure level; security recommendations; software inventory; and discovered vulnerabilities. You can also choose **Manage Tags**, **Collect Investigation Package**, **Run Anti-Virus Scan**, **Restrict App Execution**, **Isolate Machine**, or **Action Center** (see Figure 2-9).

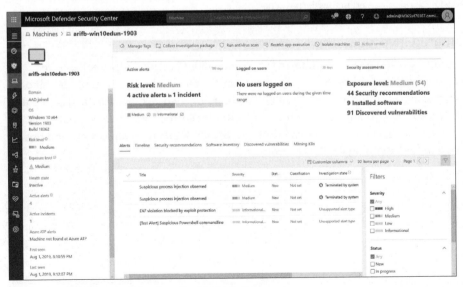

FIGURE 2-9 Viewing a machine from the Machines list

Alerts queue

The Alerts queue shows all alerts in your Microsoft Defender ATP tenant. You can sort and filter to see what alerts are associated to an incident and machine or to a user, and you can boil things down to **Severity**, **Status**, **Investigation State**, **Category**, **Assigned To**, **Detection Source**, **OS Platform**, and/or **Associated Threat**. As with most other things in the console, you can click through to get more details. Once in an alert, you can take actions, including **Manage Alert**, **View Machine Timeline**, **Open Incident Page**, and **Print Alert**, as shown in Figure 2-10.

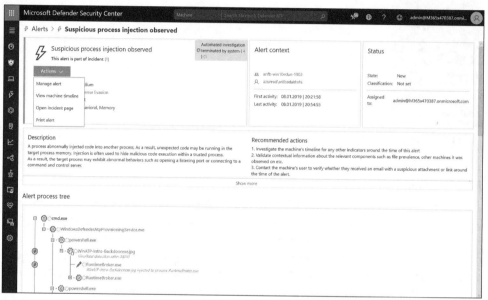

FIGURE 2-10   Viewing an alert in the Alerts queue

Automated Investigations

The Automated Investigations dashboard lists investigations automatically created by the system (see Figure 2-11). By default, it only shows you the past seven days, but you can choose an alternate time or custom date range. It lists all the automated investigations and can be filtered by **Status**, **Triggering Alert**, **Detection Source**, or **Entity**, and each investigation can be clicked to view details including the **Investigation Graph**, **Alerts**, **Machines**, **Key Findings**, **Entities**, **Log**, and **Pending Actions History**.

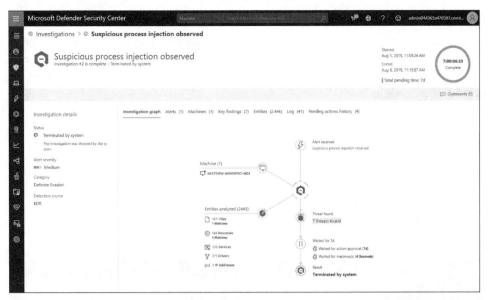

FIGURE 2-11 Viewing an Automated Investigation

Advanced Hunting

The Advanced Hunting dashboard provides an interface to create or paste queries to search data within Microsoft Defender ATP (see Figure 2-12). The Schema provides insight into what can be queried, and the Query Editor lets you create a query from scratch or paste in queries you download from GitHub or other locations. You can save and share queries for future use.

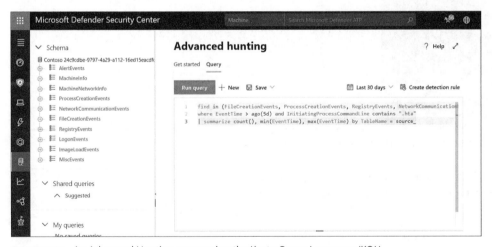

FIGURE 2-12 An Advanced Hunting query using the Kusto Query Language (KQL)

Reports

The Reports dashboard provides graphical summaries of what is going on in your environment and can be filtered like any of the other dashboards. There are two subsections under **Reports**. In the **Threat Protection** section, you can view reports on **Alert Trends** and an **Unsolved Alert Summary** that includes:

- Detection Source
- Category
- Severity
- Status
- Classification And Determination

By default, reports show the past 30 days of information, but you can select other periods or custom date ranges (see Figure 2-13).

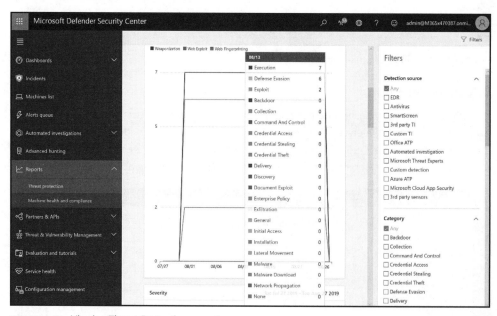

FIGURE 2-13 Viewing Threat Protection reports

In the **Machine Health And Compliance** subsection shown in Figure 2-14, you can view **Machine Trends** and **Machine Summary** for:

- Health State
- Antivirus Status
- OS Platform
- Version

FIGURE 2-14 Viewing Machine Health And Compliance reports

Partners & APIs

The Partners & APIs section includes two sections. The Partner Applications pane displays the many third-party applications that can be integrated with Microsoft Defender ATP. There are several, and more are added frequently. Several can be used to add capabilities for non-Microsoft operating systems, such as Mac or Linux; these include Bitdefender, SentinelOne, and Ziften, as shown in Figure 2-15.

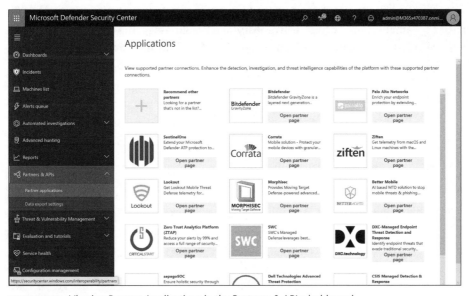

FIGURE 2-15 Viewing Partner Applications in the Partners & APIs dashboard

The Data Export Settings section is where you can choose the data export settings, which are used to push data to other applications, such as SIEMs (see Figure 2-16).

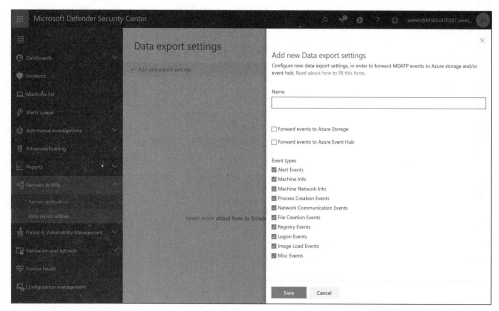

FIGURE 2-16   Add A New Data Export Settings in the Partners & APIs section

Threat & Vulnerability Management Dashboard

The Threat & Vulnerability Management Dashboard (TVM) gives administrators a risk-based, real-time way to discover vulnerabilities in their environments, prioritize them based on risk, and remediate them easily (see Figure 2-17). TVM options are **Dashboard**, **Security Recommendations**, **Remediation**, **Software Inventory**, and **Weaknesses**. The dashboard provides an overview, including the **Exposure Distribution And Configuration Score** to help administrators identify gaps and improve their security postures.

FIGURE 2-17 The Threat & Vulnerability Management Dashboard

Simulations & Tutorials

The Simulations & Tutorials section shown in Figure 2-18 includes the Evaluation Lab and a set of tutorials with simulations so that Microsoft Defender ATP administrators can work in the environment without exposing machines to actual malicious files. The Evaluation Lab lets customers try Microsoft Defender ATP using virtual machines hosted by Microsoft, while the Simulations & Tutorials section can be used against a customer's own machines for testing and learning.

FIGURE 2-18 The Simulations & Tutorials section of Microsoft Defender ATP

Service Health

Service Health is where admins go to check on the overall health of the Microsoft Defender ATP service (see Figure 2-19). If you suspect an issue with the services provided by Microsoft, you can quickly check here to see whether there is an active incident. You can also find historical information on past issues.

FIGURE 2-19   The Service Health dashboard

Machine Configuration Management

There is a lot included in the Machine Configuration Management dashboard shown in Figure 2-20. You can onboard machines and configure and apply security baselines to enrolled machines through Intune. Also, you can access the appropriate Intune section from here. Additionally, you can jump to the Machine Attack Surface Management section to help enable Windows settings or block possible vectors of attack. These powerful capabilities leverage Intune to apply a standard security posture to all machines.

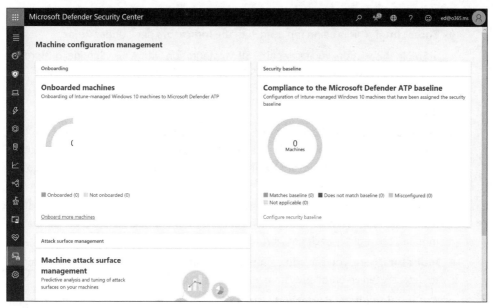

Machine configuration management

Onboarding

Onboarded machines
Onboarding of Intune-managed Windows 10 machines to Microsoft Defender ATP

Security baseline

Compliance to the Microsoft Defender ATP baseline
Configuration of Intune-managed Windows 10 machines that have been assigned the security baseline

0
Machines

■ Onboarded (0)   ■ Not onboarded (0)

Onboard more machines

■ Matches baseline (0)   ■ Does not match baseline (0)   ■ Misconfigured (0)
■ Not applicable (0)

Configure security baseline

Attack surface management

Machine attack surface management
Predictive analysis and tuning of attack surfaces on your machines

FIGURE 2-20 The Machine Configuration Management dashboard

Settings

The last section is where settings are configured. The settings are broken up into several categories, with options underneath each. They include:

- **General**
  - **Data Retention.** This is where you determine your data is stored (US, UK, or EU) and for how long it is retained (up to 180 days).
  - **Alert Notifications.** This is where you configure email alerts.
  - **Power BI Reports.** This is where you can create PowerBI dashboards.
  - **Secure Score.** This is where you can disable those features you do not want reported on Secure Score because you are addressing the topic with third-party solutions.
  - **Advanced Features.** This is where you enable advanced features, including integration with Office ATP and Azure ATP and enabling previewing features.
- **Permissions**
  - **Roles.** By default, Global Administrators and Security Administrators have full administrative rights in Microsoft Defender ATP, and Security Readers have read-only rights. If you require more granular control, you can enable RBAC and define roles here.
  - **Machine Groups.** If you need to manage different groups of machines in different ways (such as for testing) or if you need to delegate authority to a group you created in RBAC, you can create machine groups and assign permissions to them for management through Microsoft Defender ATP.

- **APIs**
    - **Threat Intel.** This is being replaced with the **Indicators** page under **Rules**.
    - **SIEM.** In this section, you can enable SIEM integration with Azure Sentinel or third-party SIEMs, and you can enable MSSP capabilities to connect to your Microsoft Defender ATP instance.
- **Rules**
    - **Custom Detections.** Custom detection rules are used to identify things that are specific to your environment. They can include Indicators of Compromise (IoCs) that you developed internally, event IDs from custom applications, or any other kind of behavior.
    - **Alert Suppression.** Suppression rules are used to mute alerts that are generated from things you just have to accept in your environment, such as a legacy app that modifies the registry each time it runs.
    - **Indicators.** Here, you can add or import file hashes, IP addresses, URLs, or domains to detect when an enrolled system attempts to access a file or a destination.
    - **Automation Allowed/Blocked Lists.** You can add code-signing certificates here for automatically blocked or allowed files.
    - **Automation Uploads.** In **File Content Analysis**, you can enable or disable the automatic upload of files for analysis within Microsoft Defender ATP, including specific file extensions, and you can enable or disable **Memory Content Analysis**. By default, both are enabled.
    - **Automation Folder Exclusions.** If you have certain proprietary applications that you do not want subject to file content analysis, you can exempt their file paths here without disabling the protection for everything else.
- **Machine Management**
    - **Onboarding.** As discussed previously, this is where you download onboarding scripts or the installers for downstream clients.
    - **Offboarding.** As discussed previously, this is where you download offboarding scripts. Make sure you note that offboarding scripts must be refreshed every 30 days and that their file name includes the "use by" date.

EXAM TIP

You should be familiar with what you can do in each of the sections of the Microsoft Defender ATP UI. If you have used Microsoft Defender ATP in production, this should be easy. However, if you are not actively using Microsoft Defender ATP, take the time to be sure you can list what is done where.

Monitoring Microsoft Defender ATP

Monitoring Microsoft Defender ATP is straightforward. If your team is actively managing endpoints, then they will likely be logged into Microsoft Defender ATP and using the console throughout their work. The Security operations dashboard is designed to surface the most useful information, making it easy to determine at a glance if any actions are required. You can see the service health, at-risk machines and users, see active alerts, and determine if any machines are having sensor issues or are not reporting to the service.

You can also integrate Microsoft Defender ATP with your SIEM. Microsoft's own SIEM— Azure Sentinel—is supported, as are both Splunk and HP ArcSight. Other SIEMs can connect using a generic connector or by using a REST API.

Skill 2.3: Implement and manage device and application protection

This objective focuses on several of the built-in protections within Microsoft Windows 10 Enterprise Edition, as well as additional protections that can be applied to applications and to data. We will first look at Windows 10 features and then move on to additional protections.

> **This skill covers how to:**
> - Plan for device protection
> - Configure and manage Windows Defender Application Guard
> - Configure and manage Windows Defender Application Control
> - Configure and manage Windows Defender Exploit Guard
> - Configure Secure Boot
> - Configure and manage Windows 10 device encryption
> - Plan for securing applications data on devices
> - Define managed apps for mobile application management (MAM)
> - Protect your enterprise data using Windows Information Protection (WIP)
> - Configure WIP policies
> - Configure Intune App Protection Policies for non-Windows devices

Plan for device protection

Windows 10 includes several features to help protect devices from malicious activity. These features can be managed by the user, they can be centrally managed using Group Policy for domain-joined systems, or they can be managed using Intune for Azure AD–joined systems. You can access the features directly by pressing the Start button, typing **device security**, and pressing **Enter**. See the Device Security dashboard in Figure 2-21.

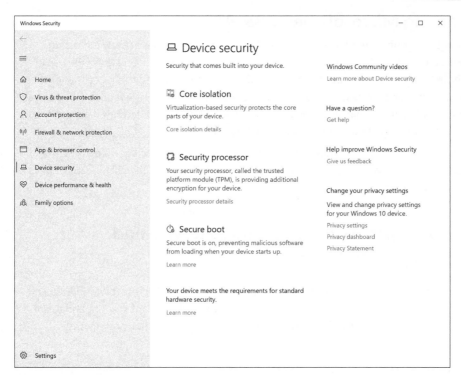

FIGURE 2-21 Device Security settings

There are three sections in the Device Security dashboard:

- **Core Isolation.** Core isolation enables Windows 10 to use virtualization to help protect your system from malicious software. Core isolation prevents attacks from inserting malicious code into high-security processes. The system performs code integrity validation and uses the Hyper-V hypervisor to maintain permissions on memory pages. This can effectively stop many types of malware from running. Enabling Core Isolation requires a reboot (see Figure 2-22).

- **Security Processor.** The Security Processor is the Trusted Platform Module (TPM) chip that is in most enterprise-class computers. The TPM is used by Windows 10 with Windows Hello for Business, BitLocker disk encryption, Secure Boot, and Health Attestation. You don't do much here unless you need to troubleshoot services that rely upon the TPM or you need to clear it before recycling a PC or reissuing it to a new user. Click the Security Processor Troubleshooting link to view TPM Error Messages or choose Clear TPM to clear the TPM, as shown in Figure 2-23.

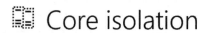

Core isolation

Security features available on your device that use virtualization-based security.

This change requires you to restart your device.

Memory integrity

Prevents attacks from inserting malicious code into high-security processes.

On

Learn more

FIGURE 2-22 Enabling Memory integrity under Core Isolation

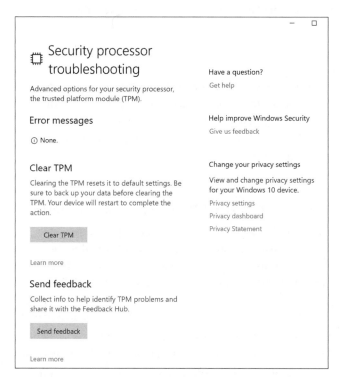

 Security processor troubleshooting

Advanced options for your security processor, the trusted platform module (TPM).

Error messages

ⓘ None.

Clear TPM

Clearing the TPM resets it to default settings. Be sure to back up your data before clearing the TPM. Your device will restart to complete the action.

Clear TPM

Learn more

Send feedback

Collect info to help identify TPM problems and share it with the Feedback Hub.

Send feedback

Learn more

Have a question?
Get help

Help improve Windows Security
Give us feedback

Change your privacy settings
View and change privacy settings for your Windows 10 device.
Privacy settings
Privacy dashboard
Privacy Statement

FIGURE 2-23 Security Processor Troubleshooting

- **Secure Boot.** Secure Boot is designed to prevent malicious code from loading during system startup. Secure Boot has no configuration, but you can verify that your system is performing secure boots on this screen. Secure boots rely upon a UEFI BIOS–compatible hardware drivers and PKI to ensure only authorized operating system components are loaded. Following is the Secure Boot sequence:

1. When the PC first boots (or is rebooted), signature databases are each checked against the platform key to ensure that the firmware is valid.

2. If the firmware is not valid, UEFI firmware initiates an OEM-specific recovery process (boot menu) to restore a trusted firmware, usually from a USB key. However, if all is well, the machine proceeds to the next step.

3. The Windows Boot Manager is checked against the database. If it fails, the firmware should boot from a backup copy of Windows Boot Manager. If this fails as well, the firmware initiates an OEM-specific recovery process.

4. Once Windows Boot Manager is running, drivers are checked as they are loaded. If any fail to have a valid signature, the Windows Recovery Environment (Windows RE) is loaded, so you can begin a repair or recovery process. However, if all goes well, the machine proceeds to the next step.

5. Windows loads the installed antimalware software (Windows Defender AV or third-party antivirus applications) that registered with Windows Security.

6. Windows finishes loading the other kernel drivers and then initializes the user mode processes.

> **IMPORTANT**
>
> Protections such as BitLocker and Secure Boot are helpful when trying to secure a system, but a malicious actor can still convince a user to do things that can put a system at risk. Limiting administrative rights, using multiple layers of security including Microsoft Defender ATP, and providing good user education are all key components of strong information security. Don't rely on any single setting or technology.

Configure and manage Windows Defender Application Guard

Windows Defender Application Guard (WDAG) uses hardware isolation to protect against attacks that start when a user visits a website hosting malware, regardless of whether that site is an attacker's site they convinced a user to visit or it is a legitimate site that an attacker has compromised. When a user accesses an untrusted site using either Internet Explorer or Microsoft Edge, the site is opened in an isolated Hyper-V based container that is kept separate from the rest of the operating system. This prevents any code the browser may run as a part of the website from accessing any other part of the system, including local storage and cached credentials. It also ensures that when the browser is closed, nothing remains from the website.

Figure 2-24 shows how isolation of Microsoft Edge with Windows Defender Application Guard works.

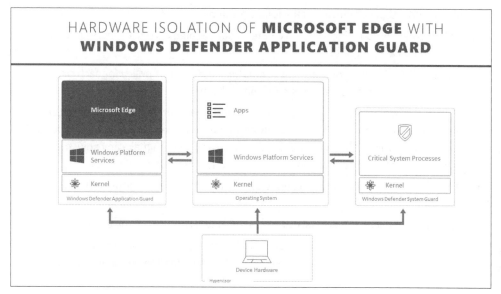

FIGURE 2-24 How Windows Defender Application Guard works

Configure and manage Windows Defender Application Control

Windows Defender Application Control (WDAC) is a feature in Windows 10 Enterprise that operates on the premise that applications are not trusted by default; instead, they must earn trust to run. It limits what applications can run in the kernel and can block unsigned binaries and scripts. It even limits PowerShell to running in Constrained Language Mode. When using WDAC, you can create multiple policies, some of which will allow software you permit to run and some of which will allow any software signed by a trusted certificate to run; also, you can block the running of other specific software, even if it is signed.

WDAC policies are created using PowerShell and can be deployed using any method that can deploy MSIs, or it can use the Intelligent Security Graph, Intune, or Group Policy. Using these controls involves four steps:

1. Review the requirements, paying attention to the hardware requirements.

2. Create groups or populations of devices based on the level of control needed. Different departments might use different applications or have different levels of security.

3. Look at the hardware and determine how many different types of systems are in the environment. WDAC applies to applications and drivers, so you might need to create different policies for the different hardware in your environment, as well as the different application needs.

4. Identify mission-critical or LOB applications in your environment that are using un-signed binaries. If they are required—but are not signed or cannot be signed—you must build a catalog file to accommodate them.

Deploying WDAC policies includes the following steps:

1. While optional, you might want to create a code-signing certificate in order to sign catalog files and policies.

2. Start with a reference computer (or computers) and create a policy for each class of machine based on hardware, business unit, or both.

3. Run the policies in Audit mode so you can determine whether all desired applications can run and any that you have explicitly chosen to block cannot run. Audit mode will log an event but will not block anything, so if necessary, you can make any adjustments to support critical/LOB applications and address any driver issues.

4. Create the catalog file for applications/drivers that must be permitted but cannot be signed.

5. Update the policies as necessary based on what was captured in the event log.

6. Deploy the updated policies in Enforce mode, testing with a small group of users or test machines to ensure you captured everything that you need to permit in your environment.

You can learn more about Windows Defender Application Control at *https://docs.microsoft. com/en-us/windows/security/threat-protection/windows-defender-application-control/ windows-defender-application-control*.

> **IMPORTANT**
>
> **WDAC will prevent you from installing any MSI directly from the Internet. To work around this, download the MSI and then run it locally.**

Configure and manage Windows Defender Exploit Guard

Windows Defender Exploit Guard (WDEG) is a combination of technologies that—together with signals from the Microsoft Intelligent Security Graph (ISG)—protect against emerging threats. The four components that make up WDEG include:

- **Attack Surface Reduction (ASR).** These controls enable an organization to block Office, script, and email-based threats.

- **Network Protection.** Blocks outbound connections from any process to untrusted hosts by FQDN or a network address.

- **Controlled Folder Access.** Blocks access to protected folders from untrusted processes.

- **Exploit Protection.** A series of exploit mitigations.

ASR can prevent Office apps from creating new executable content; can prevent Office apps from launching child processes or injecting code into a process; prevents Office macros from importing Win32 executables; and blocks obfuscated macro code. It can also block JavaScript,

VBScript, and PowerShell scripts, and it can prevent JavaScript and VBScript from downloading and executing content from the Internet.

Network protection works with the ISG to provide kernel-level protection the same way SmartScreen protects Microsoft Edge. Before a process can make an outbound connection to anything in the Internet zone (which is everything NOT in one of the other zones), the reputation for the destination is checked against the ISG. If the destination is dangerous, the connection can be killed.

Controlled Folder Access (see Figure 2-25) can block programs from accessing critical file paths, even if they are running in the context of an administrator account or system. When combined with the cloud backup protections of OneDrive for Business, users can easily recover if they inadvertently execute a piece of ransomware. By default, folders under the user's profile are protected, but you can add other folders for any application or other path that you need, and you can also configure exceptions for specific applications.

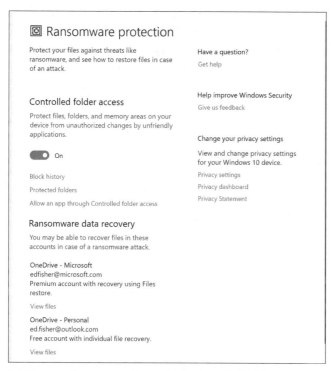

FIGURE 2-25   Ransomware Protection in Controlled Folder Access

Configure Secure Boot

Secure boot requires hardware that supports it, and it needs to be enabled in the UEFI BIOS before the operating system is installed. If you want to change Secure Boot from on to off or vice versa, you will need to reinstall the operating system after you make the change. Specific instructions for changing the settings in the UEFI BIOS can be obtained from your OEM hardware vendor, though it's typically a simple setting in the UEFI BIOS (often found in the security settings).

Configure and manage Windows 10 device encryption

Windows 10 device encryption is an enhanced version of BitLocker. With compatible hardware, and a supported version of Windows 10, you can use Windows 10 device encryption to protect your data. Device encryption can take advantage of the newer XTS-AES128 and XTS-AES256, which are both more resilient to known ciphertext attacks than AES. The best thing about Windows 10 device encryption is that with Azure AD joined machines, they will automatically encrypt drives and store the recovery keys in Azure AD.

You can view the settings for device encryption by pressing the **Start** button and typing **device encryption settings** (see Figure 2-26). If your hardware and operating system supports Device Encryption (not available with Windows 10 Home, non-UEFI hardware, or with older TPM chips), you will see it enabled already on an Azure AD–joined machine. If your machine is not Azure AD–joined, you can enable **Device Encryption** there by clicking **Turn On**. (If **Device Encryption** is enabled, you can disable it by clicking **Turn Off**.)

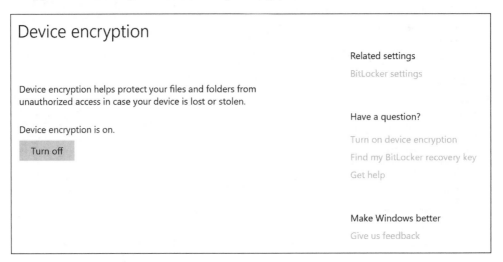

FIGURE 2-26   Device encryption in Windows 10

Plan for securing applications data on devices

When planning to secure application data on devices, you must first consider what devices will be allowed to access or store corporate data and whether they will be managed or unmanaged. Today, many organizations are still hesitant to embrace a Bring Your Own Device

(BYOD) strategy because they are concerned about corporate data on unmanaged devices, but there are many things one can do to mitigate the risks. Most requirements are focused on preventing access to data from unauthorized users and revoking access to data when an authorized user is no longer authorized to do so. To put it another way, when an employee's relationship with the company ends, the employee's access is revoked. Device encryption can be enforced on Windows systems and mobile devices along with password complexity and lockout. These protections make it more difficult for an attacker to gain access to the data, even when the attacker has physical access to the device. However, if an attacker has physical access, he or she can overcome many security measures given enough time, so remote wipe has traditionally been the approach to take. However, using BYOD remote wipe could mean wiping out a user's personal data, such as important photos or personal email, and few users are willing to take that chance. Fewer organizations want to run the risk of destroying a user's personal data.

Microsoft's approach is to use Microsoft Intune; Mobile Device Management is used for company-owned devices, and Mobile Application Management (MAM) is used to secure the application and enable secure access even when supporting a Bring Your Own Device (BYOD) environment. With MAM, you protect the specific data that a managed application uses, such as email, so that you are only focusing on the corporate data that is important to protect, rather than the overall device.

Define managed apps for mobile application management (MAM)

Mobile application management (MAM) uses Microsoft Intune to manage applications, publishing, pushing, configuring, securing, monitoring, and updating enrolled mobile devices for their users. It also enables organizations to protect data with applications even without enrollment (MAM-WE). Protected applications include the full range of Microsoft applications, such as Outlook Mobile, Teams, Word, OneDrive, and so on; protected third-party apps include Adobe Acrobat Reader, Box, Citrix Secure Mail, SAP Fiori, and more.

> **NOTE MICROSOFT INTUNE–PROTECTED APPS**
>
> You can see a complete list of supported applications at *https://docs.microsoft.com/en-us/intune/apps-supported-intune-apps*.

Intune MAM supports both Intune MDM+MAM and MAM-WE. Pushing an application requires that Intune manage the device (MDM+MAM) and that the app deployment is not restricted by the terms of the mobile app store for the device.

To manage MAM, sign in to the Azure portal and access the **Intune** blade (see Figure 2-27).

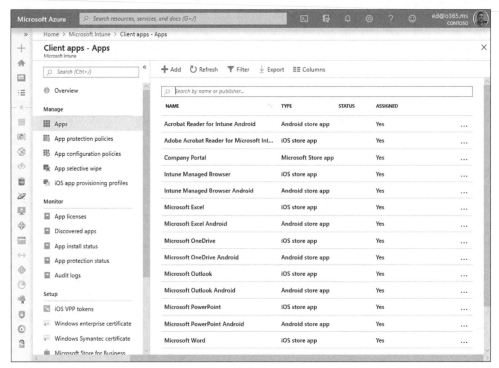

FIGURE 2-27 Client apps in Microsoft Intune

This pane is divided into four sections:

- **Manage.** This is where you can add, assign, and monitor applications, set policies, wipe data, and set up iOS provisioning profiles.
- **Monitor.** This is where you can manage licensing of apps, discover apps, check the install status, and review protection status and audit logs.
- **Setup.** This is where you manage tokens, certificates, side-loading of apps, company portal branding, and sync apps that are approved for your organization.
- **Help And Support.** This is where you can view the status of the service, troubleshoot issues, and open support requests.

Protect your enterprise data using Windows Information Protection (WIP)

Windows Information Protection (WIP) is the MAM mechanism for Windows 10 devices. Much like MAM is useful for smartphones, WIP is useful for laptops and Windows tablets. For organizations that want to support a BYOD for PCs, WIP ensures that data remains secure and can be remotely wiped; WIP also can prevent data from moving between enterprise and personal applications. WIP works with Azure Rights Management when protected data needs to move from the device, such as when a file is attached to an email, to ensure protection remains with the data. WIP provides several benefits for enterprises:

- There is a separation between personal data and enterprise data that is enforced, without requiring the user to change apps or use different logon profiles.
- Existing applications can be protected without requiring an update or rewrite.
- Corporate data can be wiped without wiping personal data.

Configure WIP policies

WIP policies can be configured with one of four different protection/management modes:

- **Block.** This mode blocks a user from moving data from a corporate to a personal app, such as copying data from a corporate email and pasting it into a personal one, sharing data in non-sanctioned locations, or with users outside the organization.
- **Allow Overrides.** This mode warns a user of any of the same actions as the Block mode, but it enables the user to continue if he or she chooses to override the policy. This is logged, so you can follow up if needed.
- **Silent.** This allows a user to do anything he or she wants to with the data, but logs when corporate data is moved to personal applications or locations as long as the policy would have let the user override when prompted. Actions that are prohibited, such as when a non-managed app tries to access WIP-protected data, are still blocked.
- **Off.** The WIP policies are turned off, and locally stored WIP-tagged data is decrypted.

You create WIP policies using Microsoft Intune by following these steps:

1. Access **Client Apps** in the **Microsoft Intune** blade.
2. Click **App Protection Policies**.
3. Click **Create Policy**.
4. Fill in the required information, as shown in Figure 2-28, and select to which apps it applies.

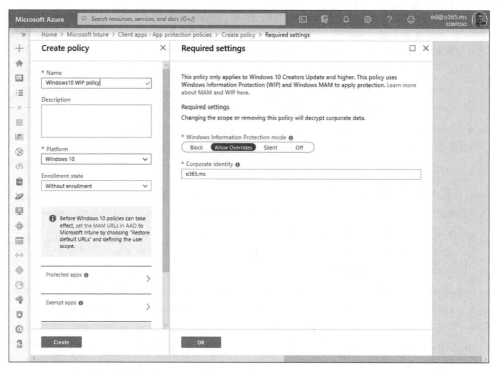

FIGURE 2-28 Creating a WIP policy

You might be prompted to set the MDM or MAM URLs in AAD and to define the user scope. These include the URLs users can visit to view the terms of use, as well as the discovery and compliance URLs. The scope can be set to **None**, **Some** (where you will select user groups), or **All**.

When adding applications, you can choose from **Recommended Apps**, **Store Apps**, and **Desktop Apps**. Recommended Apps include popular Microsoft apps frequently used by enterprises (see Figure 2-29). All necessary information is already populated when you choose one or more **Recommended Apps**.

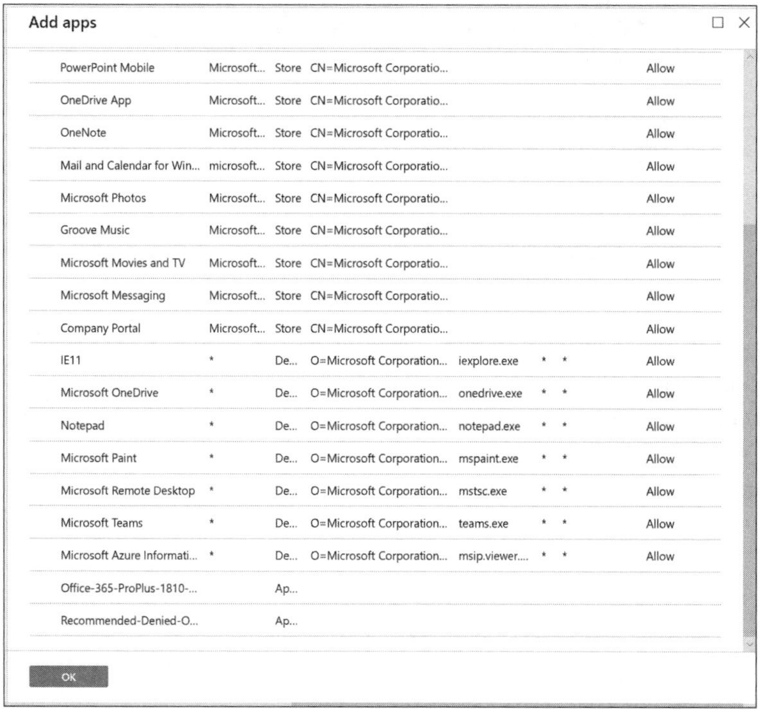

PowerPoint Mobile	Microsoft...	Store	CN=Microsoft Corporatio...					Allow
OneDrive App	Microsoft...	Store	CN=Microsoft Corporatio...					Allow
OneNote	Microsoft...	Store	CN=Microsoft Corporatio...					Allow
Mail and Calendar for Win...	microsoft...	Store	CN=Microsoft Corporatio...					Allow
Microsoft Photos	Microsoft...	Store	CN=Microsoft Corporatio...					Allow
Groove Music	Microsoft...	Store	CN=Microsoft Corporatio...					Allow
Microsoft Movies and TV	Microsoft...	Store	CN=Microsoft Corporatio...					Allow
Microsoft Messaging	Microsoft...	Store	CN=Microsoft Corporatio...					Allow
Company Portal	Microsoft...	Store	CN=Microsoft Corporatio...					Allow
IE11	*	De...	O=Microsoft Corporation...	iexplore.exe	*	*		Allow
Microsoft OneDrive	*	De...	O=Microsoft Corporation...	onedrive.exe	*	*		Allow
Notepad	*	De...	O=Microsoft Corporation...	notepad.exe	*	*		Allow
Microsoft Paint	*	De...	O=Microsoft Corporation...	mspaint.exe	*	*		Allow
Microsoft Remote Desktop	*	De...	O=Microsoft Corporation...	mstsc.exe	*	*		Allow
Microsoft Teams	*	De...	O=Microsoft Corporation...	teams.exe	*	*		Allow
Microsoft Azure Informati...	*	De...	O=Microsoft Corporation...	msip.viewer....	*	*		Allow
Office-365-ProPlus-1810-...		Ap...						
Recommended-Denied-O...		Ap...						

OK

FIGURE 2-29 Recommended Apps for a WIP policy

When entering a Store app from the Microsoft Store, you must manually enter the **Name**, **Publisher**, and **Product Name**. You can retrieve these values using the Microsoft Store for Business website and the Store for Business portal API, or you can get that information from your application developer. To look up this information, follow these steps:

1. Access the Microsoft Store for Business website at *https://businessstore.microsoft.com/ en-us/store*.

2. Search for and select the application from the website.

3. Copy the text string from the end of the application URL. It will be the last string of numbers and letters after the application name. For example, Dropbox's URL is *https:// businessstore.microsoft.com/en-us/store/details/dropbox/9wzdncrfj0pk*, so the text string you want is *9wzdncrfj0pk*.

4. Then access the Store for Business portal API at *https://bspmts.mp.microsoft.com/v1/ public/catalog/Retail/Products/########/applockerdata*, replacing the ######## with the string from the app. In this example, that would now be *https://bspmts.mp.microsoft. com/v1/public/catalog/Retail/Products/9wzdncrfj0pk/applockerdata*.

5. Your browser will display the relevant data, as shown in Figure 2-30.

{
    "packageFamilyName": "C27EB4BA.Dropbox_xbfy0k16fey96",
    "packageIdentityName": "C27EB4BA.DROPBOX",
    "windowsPhoneLegacyId": "47e5340d-945f-494e-b113-b16121aeb8f8",
    "publisherCertificateName": "CN=852D08DC-3DFB-4331-AD77-990D03FE9E36"
}

FIGURE 2-30   Viewing the Store data for the Dropbox app

6. Paste the *publisherCertificateName* into the **Publisher** field and paste the *package-IdentityName* into the **Product Name** field (see Figure 2-31). You can use any string you want for the **Name**. Under **Action**, select whether to **Allow** or **Deny** the application.

FIGURE 2-31   Adding the Dropbox application using the data retrieved from the API

7. Click **OK** when you are done.

Configure Intune App Protection Policies for non-Windows devices

The process to configure App Protection Policies for iOS and Android is similar, and it is done in the same place. You select the platform, the targeted state (MDM or MAM,) and the application, and then you set the **Data Protection Settings**, **Access Requirements**, **Launch Settings**, and **Scope** (see Figure 2-32).

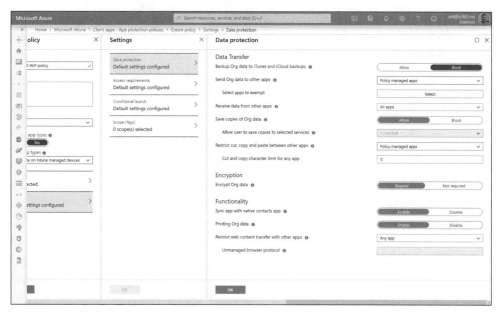

FIGURE 2-32 Data Protection settings

Skill 2.4: Implement and manage Office 365 ATP

Office 365 Advanced Threat Protection (ATP) does much more than just protect messaging. Keep that in mind as you review this material because SharePoint Online, OneDrive for Business, Microsoft Teams, and Office 365 ProPlus all benefit from the protections provided by Office 365 ATP.

Office 365 ATP is one part of Microsoft Threat Protection. It provides advanced threat protection for the SaaS applications and data that enterprises use with Office 365, and it includes advanced anti-phishing protections; Office 365 ATP also provides protection against zero-day and advanced malware through Safe Attachments, and it provides protection against malicious links in email, instant messages, and files through Safe Links. Together, these features help protect enterprises against targeted attacks and zero-day exploits, and it protects both against threats coming from outside the environment (North-South) and threats propagating within the environment (East-West). Office 365 ATP Plan 1 includes the anti-phishing, Safe Attachments, and Safe Links protections. Office 365 ATP Plan 2 adds Threat Intelligence, automation, spoof intelligence, and the Attack Simulator. Office 365 ATP P1 and P2 can be purchased as standalone offerings, and Office 365 ATP P2 is included in Office 365 E5, Microsoft 365 E5, and Office 365 E5 Security & Compliance SKUs.

This skill covers how to:

- Configure Office 365 ATP anti-phishing policies
- Define users and domains to protect with Office 365 ATP Anti-Phishing
- Configure actions against impersonation
- Configure Office 365 ATP anti-spam protection
- Enable Office 365 ATP Safe Attachments
- Configure Office 365 ATP Safe Attachments policies
- Configure Office 365 ATP Safe Links policies
- Configure Office 365 ATP Safe Links blocked URLs
- Configure Office 365 Threat Intelligence
- Integrate Office 365 Threat Intelligence with Microsoft Defender ATP
- Review threats and malware trends on the Office 365 ATP Threat Management dashboard
- Review threats and malware trends with Office 365 ATP Threat Explorer and Threat Tracker
- Create and review Office 365 ATP incidents
- Review quarantined items in ATP
- Monitor online anti-malware solutions using Office 365 ATP reports
- Perform tests using Attack Simulator

Configure Office 365 ATP anti-phishing policies

Office 365 ATP starts with configuring anti-phishing policies. These policies are used to provide additional protections against user and domain impersonation. To access these policies, go to the **Security & Compliance Portal** and follow these steps:

1. Browse to *https://protection.microsoft.com*.
2. Click **Threat Management**.
3. Click **Policy**.
4. Click the **ATP Anti-Phishing** tile.

> *IMPORTANT* **THINGS ARE CHANGING**
>
> There is more than one way to get to the Office 365 ATP policies, including through the Exchange Admin Center and the new Security Portal. At the time of this writing, when you access *https://security.microsoft.com*, select **Policies**, and then select any of the Office 365 ATP policies under **Threat Protection**, you will be redirected to the **Security & Compliance Portal** for the actual settings.

You can create one or more anti-phishing policies here. It is recommended that you have only one production policy for your organization that applies equally to all users, unless you have very specific reasons to treat different users or groups differently. Security should be consistent across all users. It's okay if you want to have a test policy for a small group of users to test new settings and have one production policy for everyone else, but you should resist the urge to have one policy for executives and another for everyone else because you could find that some things get delivered to some users but not others. Determining why this is happening can be challenging when you have multiple policies.

To create an anti-phishing policy, follow these steps:

1. Click the **Create** button.

2. Click **Name Your Policy** to give your policy an intuitive **Name** and **Description**. Consider entering your name and the date so other admins know who created this policy and when it was created. If you are editing an existing policy, add a brief note explaining your edits.

3. Click **Next**; under **Add A Condition**, use the options there to define a condition. If you want a policy to apply to the entire organization, select **The Recipient Domain Is** condition and then add all your domains, including the *.onmicrosoft.com* domains (see Figure 2-33).

4. Click **Next**, and then click **Create This Policy**.

5. Click the newly created policy to edit it.

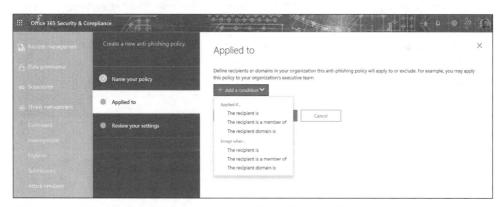

FIGURE 2-33   Adding the Applied To condition to an Office ATP anti-phishing policy

There are three sections to edit for any anti-phishing policy:

- Impersonation
- Spoof
- Advanced Settings

Impersonation settings apply to emails that are created by an attacker, which convince a recipient that the message is from someone else, such as an executive at your company, a customer, or someone from a key partner or vendor. Impersonation settings are used to apply additional scrutiny to emails that come in purporting to be from an important user in your organization or from an external domain that is significant to you, using various techniques to impersonate a sender. These can include domain names that look similar to legitimate domains (misspellings, phonetic spellings, alternative top-level domains, homoglyphs) or legitimate senders (Display Names that match other users and the like) and are a very common and very effective way to trick users into believing an email is legitimate. You can add important users in your environment (up to 60), your own domains, and any external domains that are key to your organization. Messages that are determined to be impersonation attempts can be quarantined or delivered to the user's Junk Email folder. Policy Tips can warn users about impersonation attempts when they move the message from the Junk Email folder or release it from quarantine.

Spoofing is like impersonation except that it sends emails that purport to be from a legitimate sender. Anyone can create a mail server that will identify the sender and domain as being legitimate. Sender Policy Framework (SPF), Domain-Based Message Authentication, Reporting & Conformance (DMARC), and DomainKeys Identified Mail (DKIM) can help defeat spoofing. Unfortunately, far too many domain admins do not use these methods to their fullest extent—if at all—which makes domain spoofing easy for attackers. Worse, in many cases, organizations actually want external senders to send email so that it appears to have come from the organization. This is very common in SaaS and outsourced service provider scenarios, and it is why so few companies are using SPF and DMARC as they should. These companies cannot be sure that they can identify all the various external senders who should be sending email that appears to be from their organizations. Anti-spoofing protection should be enabled, as should the **Enable Unauthenticated Sender** feature. For spoofs, the **Action** should be set to **Quarantine** because of the high likelihood of false positives.

In the **Advanced Settings**, you can increase the aggressiveness in which Office 365 ATP treats messages that might be phishing attacks. There are four levels:

- **Standard.** This level applies only to the base levels of protection from the other parts of the policy.

- **Aggressive.** This applies to messages that are considered (with either high or very high degrees of confidence) to be phishing messages.

- **More Aggressive.** This applies an even more aggressive approach in which messages—those with medium, high, and very high degrees of confidence—believed to be phishing attacks are treated the same.

- **Most Aggressive.** Even messages that have only a low degree of confidence as being phishing attempts are treated as such.

Define users and domains to protect with Office 365 ATP Anti-Phishing

The users and domains that you choose to protect with the Office 365 ATP Anti-Phishing settings are those that would significantly affect your organization if an attacker successfully spoofed a sender. Currently, the number of users you add to this policy setting is limited because of its intended purpose. Anti-phishing and anti-spoofing protections are applied to all users. These protections provide additional scrutiny to incoming emails that could appear to be from a sender requesting an action from the recipient who could significantly affect the organization. For example, a user could be bilked into authorizing a wire transfer or processing a suspect payment. If an attacker impersonated a low-level employee and sent an email to the CFO asking for a US $2M wire transfer to be executed immediately, it's unlikely the CFO would do this. However, if the attacker impersonated the CEO and asked for the same transfer, it's more likely the CFO would comply, given the number of times these attacks succeed.

You should apply these settings so that they automatically include the domains you own as well as any custom domains that are key to your organization, as shown in Figure 2-34. These could include domains you own but have not validated in your tenant; domains from other tenants you own; domains from subsidiaries or affiliated businesses; domains from key customers and financial partners; and domains in your vendor supply chain (see Figure 2-35).

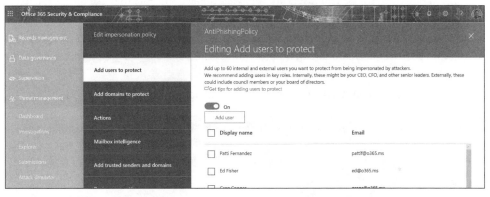

FIGURE 2-34   Editing Add Users To Protect

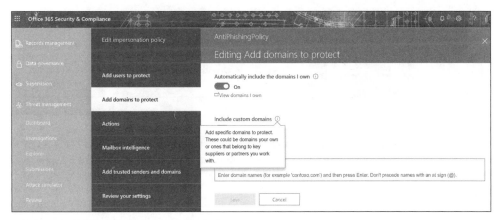

FIGURE 2-35   Editing Add Domains To Protect

Configure actions against impersonation

The actions to take when Office 365 ATP detects impersonation can be set separately for impersonated users or impersonated domains. It's recommended to quarantine any messages that appear to be impersonating a sender or a sending domain (see Figure 2-36). This prevents users from making those determinations as to whether a quarantined message is a false positive. However, this message is available for an admin in case it is needed. You should be familiar with the other options:

- **Redirect Message To Other Email Addresses.** This option allows you to redirect to another recipient, such as an information-security team or more qualified reviewer.

- **Move Message To The Recipients' Junk Email Folders.** This option is not recommended unless you can be sure your users will make the right decision.

- **Deliver The Message And Add Other Addresses To The BCC Line.** This option is not recommended unless your users are very well-trained and able to make the right choice every time.

- **Delete The Message Before It's Delivered.** This deletes the message, and there is no way to recover it. Quarantining is better in case the detection is a false positive; quarantining does not incur any additional costs.

- **Don't Apply Any Action.** This is similar to disabling the rule.

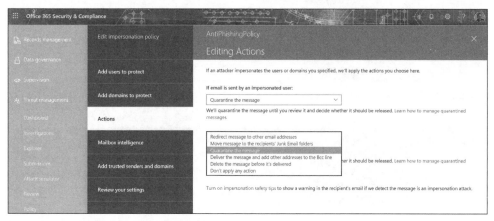

FIGURE 2-36 Editing Actions for the AntiPhishing policy

You should also enable **Impersonation Safety Tips** (see Figure 2-37) so that if a message is released from quarantine or otherwise delivered to the user, the user will see visual warnings indicating that the message is an impersonation attempt. Color-coded banners are surfaced in Outlook, Outlook Mobile, and Outlook Web Access.

FIGURE 2-37 Enabling Safety Tips for impersonation messages

Finally, note that the **Advanced Phishing Thresholds** (see Figure 2-38) settings enable aggressive actions against possible phishing attacks. The higher the threshold, the more likely that you will have false positives (FPs). As you increase the aggressiveness of the phishing thresholds, make sure you monitor, quarantine, and either adjust down or implement transport rules or Safe Sender/Safe Domain entries to allow mail from valid senders.

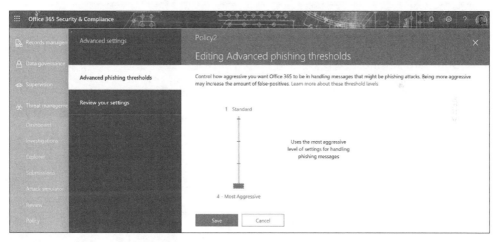

FIGURE 2-38 Editing Advanced Phishing Thresholds

Configure Office 365 ATP anti-spam protection

Though called out in the exam outline (at the time of this writing) as a part of Office 365 ATP, most of the anti-spam protections are a part of Exchange Online Protection (EOP). If you have Office 365 ATP P2, you will see the Spoof intelligence policy; otherwise, you will not. You access these in the Security & Compliance portal under Policy. As with other security mechanisms, you should aim to have a single policy that covers all users in the same way, but you can add additional policies for testing changes or if you have a strong business reason to treat different users differently. Policies include four groups of settings:

- Spam Filter Policy
- Connection Filter Policy
- Outbound Spam Filter Policy
- Spoof Intelligence Policy

The Spam Filter Policy defines how to analyze messages and how to treat those that are considered spam. As with any hygiene solution, tuning the settings will be necessary to meet the needs of your organization and the changing threat landscape. You have the option to use the standard policy or a custom policy, and you can create one or more custom policies based on your organization's needs. The standard policy is the default. The Anti-Spam Settings are not configurable, so most organizations should use a custom policy, so they can make adjustments (see Figure 2-39).

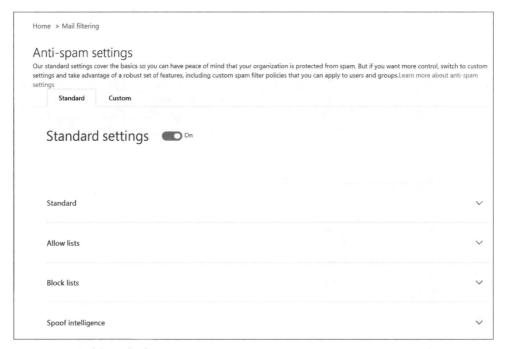

FIGURE 2-39   Anti-Spam Settings

The Default Spam Filter Policy will apply to all users unless another policy does. You can configure Spam and Bulk Actions, Allow Lists, Block Lists, and International Spam Properties. There are several settings to be familiar with in the spam and bulk options shown in Figure 2-40.

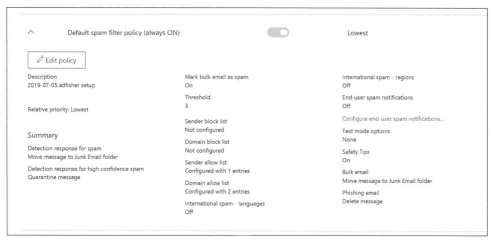

Default spam filter policy (always ON)   Lowest

✎ Edit policy

Description   Mark bulk email as spam   International spam - regions
2019-07-05 edfisher setup   On   Off

                                        Threshold   End-user spam notifications
Relative priority: Lowest   3   Off

                                        Sender block list   Configure end-user spam notifications...
                                        Not configured
Summary   Test mode options
                                        Domain block list   None
Detection response for spam   Not configured
Move message to Junk Email folder   Safety Tips
                                        Sender allow list   On
Detection response for high confidence spam Configured with 1 entries
Quarantine message   Bulk email
                                        Domain allow list   Move message to Junk Email folder
                                        Configured with 2 entries
                                                                             Phishing email
                                        International spam - languages   Delete message
                                        Off

FIGURE 2-40 Default Spam Filter Policy

REAL WORLD **TO JUNKMAIL OR TO QUARANTINE? THAT'S A GOOD QUESTION!**

By default, Exchange Online Protection (EOP) will deliver spam to the user's Junkmail Folder (JMF) rather than to quarantine it, like many competing products do. EOP even suffers in certain third-party evaluations because of this issue, even though quarantining the message is as simple as choosing to do so from a drop-down menu. Having been a messaging admin for several years, I'd much rather users sort their own junk mail than to have them open a ticket every time they think something was blocked "by the firewall." However, if you want to quarantine messages or have users receive a daily summary email to release their own spam from quarantine, then EOP can accommodate you with a drop-down menu selection where you set the frequency of user spam notifications. If spam is already in a user's JMF, the user just needs to drag it to the inbox and mark it as not being junk. Of course, high-confidence spam and phishing should not be delivered to a user's JMF. Whether you quarantine or delete is up to you.

Use caution when configuring Allow lists. You can add SMTP addresses or entire domains to a "whitelist" to permit senders to send without processing for spam or bulk. Because validating SPF records is part of processing for spam, if you add a sender to the **Allow** list, you're letting anyone send from that address without confirming their identities.

Take time to adjust the **Spam Properties**. The default settings are relatively low, and if you don't strengthen them, a lot of spam will be delivered, especially when compared to other products that block more spam by default. In particular, as shown in Figure 2-41, make sure you enable the following:

- SPF Record: Hard Fail
- Conditional Sender ID Filtering: Hard Fail
- NDR Backscatter

FIGURE 2-41   Spam Properties

Spam filtering requires monitoring and tuning to find the settings that work best for your organization. Don't just set and forget these.

Enable Office 365 ATP Safe Attachments

Office 365 Safe Attachments check attachments in email and files shared through SharePoint Online, OneDrive for Business, and Microsoft Teams to ensure they are not malicious by evaluating how the attachments act when opened in a hypervisor environment. Rather than relying upon signatures, Office ATP analyzes the attachments to confirm they are safe.

To enable policies, you must assign licenses to users, create a policy, and apply that policy to the user, to a group to which they belong, or to a domain in which they have an email address.

Configure Office 365 ATP Safe Attachments policies

Configuring the Safe Attachments policy includes enabling ATP for SharePoint, OneDrive, and Microsoft Teams and configuring how it is to handle attachments in email. Settings for Office 365 ATP Safe Attachments in email include the following and are shown in Figure 2-42:

- **Off.** No action is taken.
- **Monitor.** Detections are logged, but malicious files are still delivered.

- **Block.** Malicious messages and their attachments are blocked.
- **Replace.** Messages are delivered, but malicious attachments are replaced with a text file noting that the files were malicious and removed.
- **Dynamic Delivery.** This functions like the Replace setting, but the message is delivered immediately, while the attachment is scanned. Safe attachments are reattached to the message, while malicious ones are blocked and a text file noting the blocked attachments is attached.

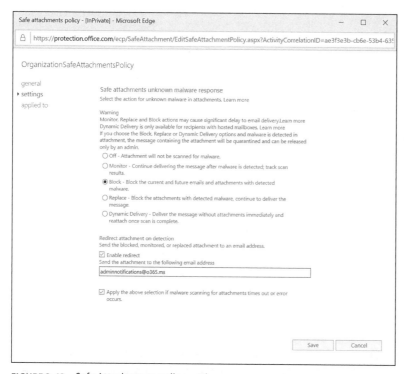

FIGURE 2-42   Safe Attachments policy settings

Configure Office 365 ATP Safe Links policies

Safe Links checks links in emails and attachments to ensure that they do not link to a malicious site that is hosting malware or is set up to attempt phishing. The service checks the link at the time the message is received, and for messages in email, the service rewrites the link so that the user is directed to the service again when it is clicked. Messages in attachments are checked, but their links are not rewritten. In either case, the message and its links are maintained so that if the link later becomes malicious, the service can automatically remove messages that were previously delivered to Exchange Online mailboxes using the Zero-Hour Auto Purge (ZAP) feature.

Like Safe Attachments, Safe Links needs to be enabled, and a policy must be applied to recipients based on their email addresses, group memberships, or email domains (see Figure 2-43). There are two settings for Safe Links:

- **Policies That Apply To The Entire Organization.** This setting configures how the Safe Links service is used by Office clients when there are links in files, including Word documents, Excel spreadsheets, and PowerPoint presentations. This setting also applies to the full Office ProPlus suite, the mobile apps, and the Office web apps.

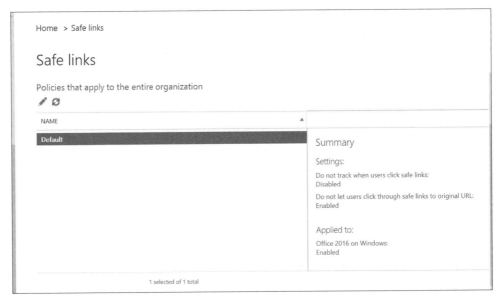

FIGURE 2-43 Safe Links organization settings

You can apply these settings to all clients, choose whether to track user clicks, and whether the block page presents the user with an option to visit a site that Safe Links has identified as malicious. Note that these settings apply to the entire organization and cannot be modified for different recipients.

- **Policies That Apply To Specific Recipients.** This includes settings for links in emails (see Figure 2-44). While you can have different policies for different groups of users, it is recommended to have a single policy that applies to all users, if possible. These settings include turning the policy on or off; applying real-time scanning and delaying delivery until the scan completes; applying Safe Links scanning to internal email; whether to track user clicks; and whether to allow users to click through the warning page. You can also configure links that should not be rewritten, such as those for internal websites or IDP-initiated sign-ins.

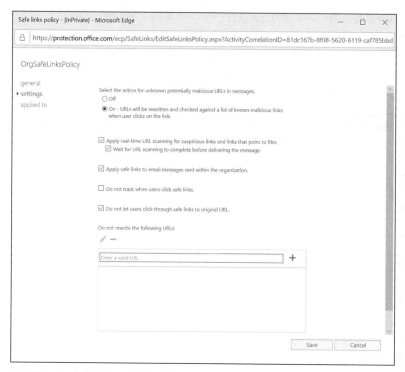

FIGURE 2-44   Safe Links policy settings

Configure Office 365 ATP Safe Links blocked URLs

You can also enter a list of URLs that you want blocked across the organization. Wildcards are supported. The service will return the block page for any link in any client that uses Safe Links. Note that this does not block the user from entering the URL into his or her browser directly or clicking the search results in a search engine. It only applies to links in documents.

Configure Office 365 Threat Intelligence

Office 365 Threat Intelligence (TI) used to be a separately licensed product but is now included in Office 365 ATP Plan 2 (see Figure 2-45). It includes both threat investigation and response capabilities:

- **Threat Management.** You use this dashboard to see information about current threats.
- **Investigations.** You use this to view Automated Investigations.
- **Explorer.** You use this to view and analyze threats.
- **Submissions.** You this to submit mail and files for Microsoft review or to see user submissions.

- **Review.** You use this to see Quarantine and review users who may have been inadvertently sending out spam.

Access to Office 365 TI requires the user to be a global administrator, a security administrator, or a security reader, or the user must have a custom RBAC role. You can access Office 365 TI in the Security & Compliance Center at *https://protection.office.com*.

FIGURE 2-45 The Threat Intelligence Dashboard

Integrate Office 365 Threat Intelligence with Microsoft Defender ATP

To integrate Office 365 TI with Microsoft Defender ATP, do the following:

1. In the Security & Compliance portal, choose **Threat Management** > **Explorer**.

2. In the upper-right corner, click **WDATP Settings**.

> **NOTE TWO THINGS TO BE AWARE OF**
>
> As you may recall, Microsoft Defender ATP used to be called Windows Defender ATP. That name still persists in some locations, including in Office 365 (at the time of this writing). Also, you might not be able to see the button until you collapse the menu at the left.

3. Set the **Connect to Windows ATP** switch to **On**, as shown in Figure 2-46.

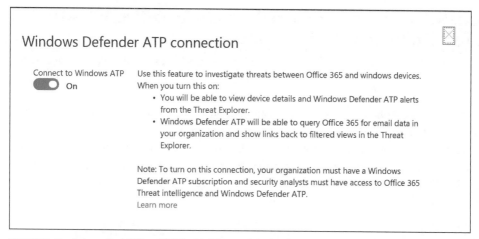

Windows Defender ATP connection

Connect to Windows ATP   Use this feature to investigate threats between Office 365 and windows devices.
On   When you turn this on:
                           • You will be able to view device details and Windows Defender ATP alerts
                             from the Threat Explorer.
                           • Windows Defender ATP will be able to query Office 365 for email data in
                             your organization and show links back to filtered views in the Threat
                             Explorer.

                           Note: To turn on this connection, your organization must have a Windows
                           Defender ATP subscription and security analysts must have access to Office 365
                           Threat intelligence and Windows Defender ATP.
                           Learn more

FIGURE 2-46   Integrating Office 365 TI with Microsoft Defender ATP

Review threats and malware trends on the Office 365 ATP Threat Management dashboard

The Office 365 ATP Threat Management dashboard surfaces information that security and messaging administrators will find useful, including how Office 365 ATP is protecting their environments, identifying the common threats, and identifying the most-targeted users. Each panel contains summary information and several options you can click through to get to the details. You access the Office 354 ATP Threat Management dashboard shown in Figure 2-47 by browsing to *https://protection.office.com*, expanding Threat Management in the left menu, and clicking **Dashboard**.

FIGURE 2-47   The Office 365 ATP Threat Management dashboard

Review threats and malware trends with Office 365 ATP Threat Explorer and Threat Tracker

Office 365 ATP Plan 1 comes with real-time detections, while Office 365 ATP Plan 2 comes with the Threat Management Explorer. Both do essentially the same thing, which is to provide your security operations center or security admins with the ability to investigate and respond to threats in your environment. You can view malware detections, view information about phishing URLs sent to your users, view emails, and more. You can view delivered email that has been submitted as spam or phishing by your users, and you can view detected malware and phishing incidents. Using the search feature, you can search email by Sender, Recipient, Subject, URL Contained In The Message, Message ID, and more; also, you can view information about the message (see Figure 2-48).

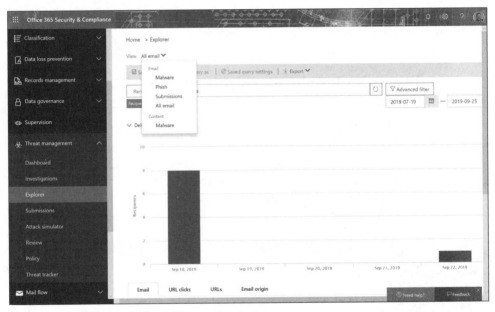

FIGURE 2-48   Office 365 ATP Threat Management Explorer

When viewing a message, you can take actions directly upon it, including deleting it, moving it to the user's inbox, launching an investigation, and more (see Figure 2-49).

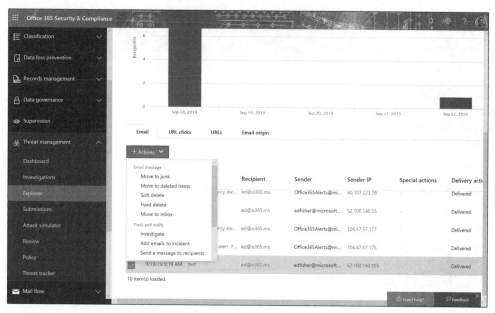

FIGURE 2-49 Viewing a message in Explorer

Threat trackers are widgets that can provide more information on global threats to keep administrators informed about what is happening across cybersecurity, including new malware or phishing campaigns. It can also view saved queries and update them. Threat trackers require Office 365 ATP Plan 2.

Create and review Office 365 ATP incidents

Office 365 ATP incidents enable administrators to track phishing and malware campaigns in their environments, to see what is targeting their users, and to take actions as appropriate. You access incidents in the **Security & Compliance portal** by navigating to **Threat Management** in the **Review** section and clicking the **Incidents** tab. Incidents are opened when a user reports a message as being spam or a phishing attempt. Also, incidents are opened when Safe Links blocks a URL as malicious, but a user chooses to click the link despite the warning (assuming you have not disabled that ability). You can view submissions, the action logs, and the scope of the incident, and you can edit or delete the submissions (see Figure 2-50).

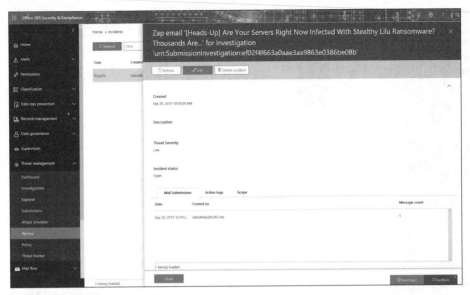

FIGURE 2-50 Reviewing an incident

Review quarantined items in ATP

In the **Review** section, you can also view the Office 365 ATP quarantine details (see Figure 2-51). This is where administrators can see messages and files that are quarantined, rather than delivered. You can view either emails or files (from SharePoint Online or OneDrive for Business), and you can take actions on those items in quarantine, including releasing, downloading, or deleting it. You can choose **Release**, **View Headers**, **Preview**, **Remove (Delete)**, **Download**, or **Submit A Message**.

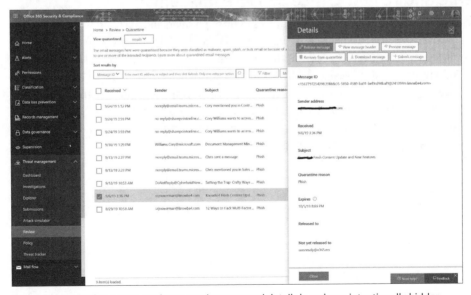

FIGURE 2-51 Viewing a message in quarantine; personal details have been intentionally hidden.

Monitor online anti-malware solutions using Office 365 ATP reports

Office 365 ATP reports are found in the Reports Dashboard and include graphical reports that include insights and recommendations for your environment. They include reports on what users are being targeted by phishing campaigns; spoofed domains; user and domain imper-sonations; malware detections; top senders and recipients; and more. Reports can be viewed ad hoc, or they can be scheduled for regular delivery (see Figure 2-52).

FIGURE 2-52   Scheduling the Sent And Received Email Report

Perform tests using Attack Simulator

Office 365 Advanced Threat Protection Plan 2 includes the Attack Simulator, which at the time of this writing, includes three tools for assessing the security of your environment by running attacks against it:

- Spear phishing (credentials harvest)
- Brute-force password attack (dictionary attack)
- Password spray attack

Spear phishing (credentials harvest)

A spear-phishing attack is a targeted attempt to acquire sensitive information, such as usernames, passwords, and credit card information, by masquerading as a trusted entity. This attack will use a URL to attempt to obtain usernames and passwords. You can create phishing messages using one of the included templates, or you can create your own phishing messages using the built-in editor. To create an attack, click the **Launch Attack** button and follow the steps in the wizard.

NOTE **MULTIFACTOR AUTHENTICATION IS REQUIRED**

Before you can launch any of the attacks from the Attack Simulator console, you must enable multifactor authentication (MFA) for your account. At the time of this writing, only Azure MFA is supported. If you do not use Azure MFA or a third-party MFA, you will not be able to use the Attack Simulator unless you create a cloud-only account and enable MFA for it. You can find the Attack Simulator in the Security & Compliance Center at *https://protection.office.com* by choosing **Threat management** > **Attack Simulator**.

There are five steps to create a spear phishing attack in the Attack Simulator:

1. Give the attack a meaningful name, as you can reuse the attack later if needed. If you want to use an existing template, select it here; otherwise, you will create a new message in step 4.

2. Pick the accounts to target, either from the **Address Book** or by importing their email addresses from a text file, one email address per line.

3. Fill out the specific details for the phishing message (see Figure 2-53):

   - **From [Name].** Who the message should appear to be from
   - **From [Email].** The sender's email address
   - **Phishing Login Server.** The phishing login URL
   - **Custom Landing Page URL.** The URL users to whom it should be directed if they attempt to log in
   - **Subject.** The email subject

4. Compose your phishing email using HTML or edit the selected template if desired (see Figure 2-54). You can embed the corporate logo or other graphics to make the message appear genuine.

5. Click Finish to complete.

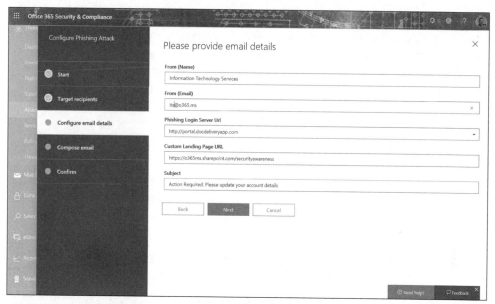

FIGURE 2-53 Configuring email details

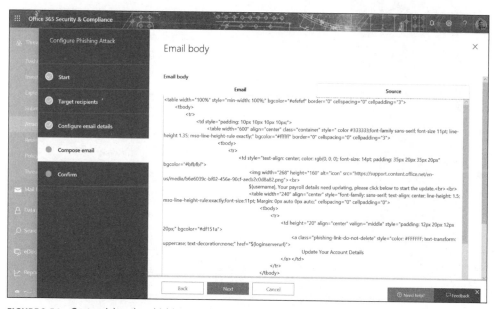

FIGURE 2-54 Customizing the phishing email template

The spear phishing messages are directly injected into the targeted users' mailboxes. If the user clicks the link, it is recorded, and if the user provides credentials, that is also recorded, so you can determine which users require further training.

Brute-force password attack (dictionary attack)

A brute-force password attack, also called a dictionary attack, is used to assess whether users are selecting strong passwords or whether they are selecting passwords that can be easily guessed by using an automated attack. You can create your own dictionary of passwords, or you can upload one that you have downloaded from the Internet. To launch a brute-force password attack, follow these four steps to create an attack in the Attack Simulator, as shown in Figure 2-55:

1. Give the attack a meaningful name, as you can reuse the attack later if you need. Then click **Next**.

2. Pick the accounts to target, either from the **Address Book** or by importing their email addresses from a text file, one email address per line. Then click **Next**. (Note that targets must have an Exchange Online mailbox.)

3. You can either enter passwords to use, one at a time, or upload a password list. The password list cannot be larger than 10MB, and it must be a plain text file, one password per line, with a hard return after each line. Then click **Next**.

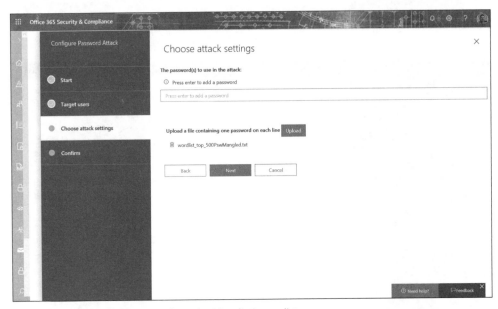

FIGURE 2-55 Brute-force password attack with a dictionary list

4. Then click **Finish** to launch the attack.

Depending upon how many users and the size of the password file you used, the attack might take some time to complete. You can click the **Refresh** button to update the status, and you can choose to terminate the attack if it still shows in progress. Once it is complete, you can view the **Attack Details** to see the results.

Password spray attack

The final attack in the Attack Simulator is the password spray attack. In a password spray attack, a list of passwords is used against one or more accounts, where the passwords meet complexity requirements but are not strong passwords. The attacker usually takes a "low and slow" approach to prevent tripping any bad password thresholds designed to protect against brute-force attempts. Password spray attacks take much longer to run, but they can go undetected and have a 1 percent average success rate. That might not sound like much, but in an organization of 1,000 users, an attacker will, on average, successfully compromise 10 users. They only need one to begin a lateral movement or internal phishing attack. When assessing your users, choose passwords that might have significance to your organization or your location, such as a department name or the name of the local professional sports team.

There are four steps to launch a password spray attack in the Attack Simulator:

1. Give the attack a meaningful name, as you can reuse the attack later if needed. Then click **Next**.

2. Pick the accounts to target, either from the **Address Book** or by importing their email addresses from a text file, one email address per line. Note that users must have an Exchange Online mailbox. Then click **Next**.

3. Enter the password you want to assess against your users. Note, you cannot import a list with this attack, and you can only use a single password at a time, even though the UI implies you can use more than one password.

4. Click **Finish** to run the attack.

You can view the results of the attack to see if any of the targeted users had the selected password, as shown in Figure 2-56.

FIGURE 2-56 Attack details for a password spray attack

Skill 2.5: Implement Azure Sentinel for Microsoft 365

Azure Sentinel provides intelligent security analytics for your entire enterprise, including cloud and on-premises infrastructure. Azure Sentinel is frequently compared to other security information and event management (SIEM) solutions, and thus it is more of a next-generation SIEM because it includes the ability to respond automatically to events using Playbooks, bringing security orchestration automated response (SOAR) capabilities to your organization. Running as a service within Azure, Azure Sentinel provides cloud-scale capabilities with artificial intelligence, threat feeds from Microsoft and other organizations, advanced hunting capabilities, and response capabilities across both your cloud services and on-premises infrastructure. Azure Sentinel can ingest logs from a variety of sources and in a variety of formats, and it does not cost anything when data is ingested from Office 365 audit logs, Azure activity logs, and from Microsoft Threat Protection solutions.

In this chapter, you learned about all the capabilities included in Microsoft Threat Protection, and which align to the five objectives for the exam. You saw how they address protecting a hybrid organization, how they protect devices, how they protect applications, and how they protect the SaaS applications and data within Office 365.

> **This skill covers how to:**
> - Plan and implement Azure Sentinel
> - Configure Playbooks in Azure Sentinel
> - Manage and monitor Azure Sentinel
> - Respond to threats in Azure Sentinel

Plan and implement Azure Sentinel

Azure Sentinel can ingest data from a variety of sources and through a variety of means, including syslog and Common Event Format (CEF) format. While data from Office 365, Azure, and Microsoft Threat Protection can all be ingested at no cost, data ingested from applications or network devices can begin to incur costs very quickly. That means having an idea of just how much data a syslog feed from your firewall will create daily is important to estimate costs. Azure Sentinel can use a charge-as-you-go or a pre-commit model, so if you have an idea of how much data you want to ingest, you should plan around what makes the best economic sense for your organization. See *https://azure.microsoft.com/en-us/pricing/details/azure-sentinel/* for more on pricing.

If you want to start with what you can ingest for free and move up from there, you can jump right in. To implement Azure Sentinel, you need the following:

- An active Azure subscription
- A Log Analytics workspace

- At least Contributor permissions to the Azure subscription

- At least Contributor or Reader permissions on the resource group to which the work-space belongs

If you meet those prerequisites, the next step is to enable Azure Sentinel:

1. Sign in to the Azure portal at *https://portal.azure.com*.

2. If you have access to more than one Azure subscription, make sure you select the correct subscription from the drop-down menu.

3. In the search field, type **Azure Sentinel** and select it, as shown in Figure 2-57.

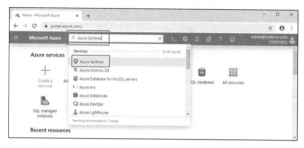

FIGURE 2-57   Finding Azure Sentinel in the Azure portal

4. Select **Add**.

5. Select the existing workspace or create a new one if you prefer.

6. Select **Add Azure Sentinel**.

Once you have added Azure Sentinel, you need to connect data sources:

1. Click Data Connectors.

2. Select the data connector you want to add to your Azure Sentinel workspace.

3. Then click **Open Connector Page** to configure the connector, as shown in Figure 2-58.

FIGURE 2-58   Adding the Azure Advanced Threat Protection connector to Azure Sentinel

4. Repeat the process for each connector you want to add.

Once connectors are set up, Azure Sentinel will begin to ingest data from the configured sources. Logs are accessible through the built-in dashboards, and you can query the data using Log Analytics.

Configure Playbooks in Azure Sentinel

Azure Sentinel Playbooks are a collection of procedures that can automatically be performed in response to an alert raised in Azure Sentinel from any of the configured data sources. This enables you to automate response actions, though you can also manually run a Playbook at will. They are created as a Logic App. You can create and manage Playbooks in the Azure Sentinel portal:

1. Log in to *https://portal.azure.com* and access Azure Sentinel by searching for **Azure Sentinel** and selecting it when it appears, or you can click the **Azure Sentinel** button at the top.

2. Under **Configuration**, click **Playbooks**.

3. Click the **Add Playbook** button to add a new Playbook. This will open a new Logic App tab.

4. In the **Basics** pane, choose the **Subscription** and **Resource Group** for the new Playbook.

5. Give the Logic App (Playbook) a name, select the region in which it will run from the **Location** drop-down menu, and select whether to use Log Analytics by toggling the **Log Analytics** button to **On** or **Off**. Finally, click **Create**.

6. The Logic App Designer will load, where you can choose a template to use or create a new blank Playbook.

7. In the **Search All Connectors And Triggers** field, enter **Azure Sentinel**.

8. Select **When A Response To An Azure Sentinel Alert Is Triggered** and click **Finish**.

9. Choose your newly created Playbook and use the *Get entities* function to select what you are interested in, such as an account or an IP address.

10. Now you can create an action or enter a condition, exception, or multiples to define what you want to happen and when.

Manage and monitor Azure Sentinel

As you begin to connect more data sources to Azure Sentinel, you will begin to ingest data that will incur additional charges. While you might be able to estimate the volume of data from a previous solution, you will also want to monitor your data ingestion during your initial free trial and on an ongoing basis to ensure you understand what charges you might be incurring and to evaluate whether you want to move to a reserved commitment rather than a pay-as-you-go arrangement. You can view your daily data ingestion in the Azure Sentinel portal:

1. From the left side of the Azure Sentinel portal, choose **Settings**.
2. Select the **Pricing** tab.
3. On the right side, you can view the **Data Ingestion** over the last month, as well as the **Data Retained** over the last month.

While you can use pay-as-you-go plan on a per-gigabyte basis, significant discounts start at 100GB per day and move up to 500GB per day. If your daily ingestion averages a volume that maps to a discounted tier, you can select the tier to obtain the discount. If you exceed the daily rate, you are charged at the per-gigabyte rate only for the volume that exceeds the daily rate. You do not get a credit for data under the chosen tier, so monitor your volume each month. Microsoft allows you to change tiers each month as your needs change, moving up or down as you need.

Respond to threats in Azure Sentinel

Once you have created a Playbook, you can choose to either manually run it or set up automation. Follow these steps to run a Playbook manually:

1. Access the **Incidents** page.
2. Select the incident and click the **View Full Details** button.
3. Select the **Alerts** tab and click the specific alert you want.
4. Scroll to the far right and click **View Playbooks**.
5. Select the Playbook you want to run.

Follow these steps to run a Playbook automatically:

1. Select the alert that you want to automatically trigger a Playbook.
2. Click **Edit Alert Rule** and scroll down to **Real-Time Automation**.
3. From the **Triggered Playbooks** drop-down menu, select the Playbook you want to run.
4. Click **Save**.

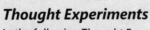

Thought Experiments

In the following Thought Experiments, apply what you've learned in this chapter. You can find answers to these questions in the "Thought Experiment Answers" section at the end of this chapter.

Using Azure ATP

You are the security administrator of Contoso. You want to implement Azure Advanced Threat Protection to help protect your organization. You want to make sure that you can assign certain tasks to members of your team using the approach of least privilege.

1. What built-in roles can you use to administer Azure ATP?
2. What are the minimum rights necessary for a user to install the Azure ATP agent on domain controllers?
3. What role would you assign to members of the help desk who need to monitor alerts?

Using Microsoft Defender ATP

You are the security administrator of Contoso. You want to use Microsoft Defender ATP to protect your organization from advanced threats.

1. What operating systems can be protected by Microsoft Defender ATP?
2. What other products can you integrate with Microsoft Defender ATP?
3. What levels of access might you need to grant administrative users of Microsoft Defender ATP?

Device Protection

You are the security administrator for Contoso corporation. You need to ensure your Windows 10 workstations are protected against threats.

1. What are the hardware requirements to support BitLocker?
2. How can you protect corporate data on personally owned (BYOD) devices?
3. How can you ensure that data can be viewed, but not edited, printed, or copied?

Protecting users from phishing attacks

You are the security administrator for Contoso. Your users are being targeted by phishing attacks in emails sent from outside the organization. You need to ensure your users do not fall victim to phishing attacks.

1. What is the first line of defense against phishing attacks in email?

2. What tool can you use in Office 365 Advanced Threat Protection Plan 2 to help educate your users about phishing attacks?

3. What can you add to messages identified as phishing attacks in case a message is released to users even after being identified as a phish?

Using Office 365 Threat Intelligence

You are the Office 365 global admin for Contoso. You want to maximize the protections for your users and ensure you are aware of new threats as soon as possible.

1. What tools can you use in Office 365 Advanced Threat Protection to help educate and inform users?

2. How can you monitor when users report spam and phishing messages that they receive?

3. What can you use to see what new attacks are occurring online?

Thought Experiment Answers

Following are answers to the questions posed in the Thought Experiments section of this chapter.

Using Azure ATP

1. Remember, there are three RBAC roles in Azure ATP: Administrators, Users, and Viewers.

2. You must be a domain admin to install things onto domain controllers.

3. To monitor, you only need an Azure ATP Viewers membership.

Using Microsoft Defender ATP

1. Microsoft Defender ATP can be used to protect supported operating systems from Windows 7 to Windows 10, Windows Server 2008 R2 to Windows Server 2019, and Mac OSX.

2. You can also protect Mac, Linux, iOS, and Android using partner applications, though you should expect to see first-party capabilities for these in the near future.

3. To administer Microsoft Defender ATP, you need to make users Global Administrators or Security Administrators or set up RBAC.

Device Protection

1. BitLocker requires a TPM version 1.2 or later chip.

2. You can use MAM or AIP to protect data on unmanaged devices.

3. You can use MAM to limit what can be done with data in managed applications, or you can use AIP to restrict what can be done with data.

Protecting users from phishing attacks

1. Exchange Online Protection is the first line of defense against phishing attacks.

2. Administrators can use the Attack Simulator to help assess and drive awareness of phishing attacks with their users.

3. Safety Tips can be used to warn users of suspect mail, even if the mail is allowed to be delivered to their inboxes.

Using Office 365 Threat Intelligence

1. Administrators can use the Attack Simulator to educate and inform users about phishing and password attacks.

2. Admins can use the Submissions pane to see what users are reporting about phishing and spam messages they receive.

3. Administrators can use the Threat Explorer/Threat Tracker to view what is going on across the Internet that is related to new attacks.

CHAPTER 3

Implement and manage information protection

Information protection in Microsoft 365 involves several features and tools we'll cover in this chapter. Microsoft's offerings, such as comprehensive data loss prevention (DLP) tools and Cloud App Security, provide your organization with a robust and diverse array of protection and administrative options. These options can track file activity down to matching keywords in contents to apply appropriate protection or to tracking and governing your organization's third-party app usage and activity, such as for Dropbox Business.

Skills in this chapter:

- Skill 3.1: Secure data access within Office 365
- Skill 3.2: Manage Azure Information Protection (AIP)
- Skill 3.3: Manage Data Loss Prevention (DLP)
- Skill 3.4: Implement and manage Microsoft Cloud App Security

Skill 3.1: Secure data access within Office 365

This module will cover what administrators need to know about managing Customer Lockbox for support issues, working with Office 365 apps and services to limit the risk of data loss, and setting up sharing with other organizations using B2B abilities. Knowing these three components of securing an environment protects your organization in external support, as well as internal and external collaboration scenarios.

This skill covers how to:

- Implement and manage Customer Lockbox
- Configure data access in Office 365 collaboration workloads
- Configure B2B sharing for external users

Implement and manage Customer Lockbox

Customer Lockbox empowers administrators to limit the amount of time Microsoft support engineers can have access to your organization's data and provide formal approval prior to allowing access. Support engineers' work in your environment is always logged for auditing purposes, but Customer Lockbox provides an additional layer of security and peace of mind. Customer Lockbox is included in Office 365 and Microsoft 365 E5 plans, but it can also be purchased as an add-on feature to other plans.

To implement Customer Lockbox, an administrator should follow these steps:

1. Go to the Microsoft 365 admin center at *https://admin.microsoft.com*.

2. Select **Settings** > **Org Settings** > **Security & Privacy** > **Customer Lockbox** (as shown in Figure 3-1).

3. Check the **Require Approval For All Data Access Requests** box and click **Save Changes**.

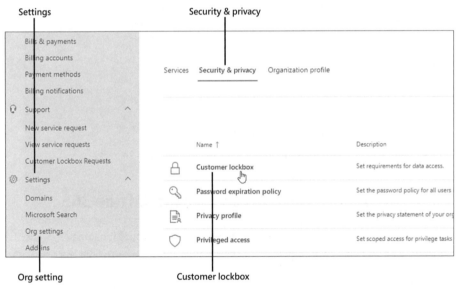

FIGURE 3-1 The steps required to access Customer Lockbox settings from the Microsoft 365 admin center

Once enabled, you'll be able to monitor and manage Custom Lockbox requests from the Microsoft 365 admin center's **Support** node. Users must be a Global Administrator or have the Customer Lockbox Access Approver role assigned to them in order to manage the requests that will come through.

If you need to audit previous Customer Lockbox activity, you can use the Security & Compliance center's **Audit Log Search**. To do this, you would run a new search with nothing configured other than the date range for which you're auditing. Follow these steps once the results are loaded:

1. Filter the **Activity** column by the text **Set-AccessToCustomerDataRequest** to find approval activities.

2. Filter the **User** column to **Microsoft Operator** to find Microsoft engineer activities.

Configure data access in Office 365 collaboration workloads

Each Office 365 app and service has its own settings that can be configured to protect data access within that app and service. There are also global settings, many of which we're covering throughout this book. This section focuses on a few global tasks you can do for all apps and services as well as at the Office 365 workload or app level to protect data access for your users and devices.

First, Microsoft recommends that when you grant an administrator role, that user should be assigned to a separate user account that is to be used exclusively for administration, instead of allowing one user to have the ability to do both administration and end user functions from the same account. Administrator roles should be protected by MFA and conditional access policies. It's also a good idea to have administrators consistently use one device for administrative work.

Second, consider creating emergency access accounts in the event administrative access is lost under unforeseen circumstances. You can read tips and guidance for accomplishing this at *https://docs.microsoft.com/en-us/azure/active-directory/users-groups-roles/directory-emergency-access*.

There are several Azure AD features and capabilities you can enable to better configure data access in Office 365 collaboration workloads. Some of these we've already covered and include the following:

- Self-service password reset (SSPR)
- Multifactor authentication (MFA)
- Conditional access
- Azure AD groups
- Device registration
- Azure AD Identity Protection

Keep in mind that Intune can be used for both device and app management, securing your users collaborating on the go via the Office 365 mobile apps.

Typically, your protection configuration for Microsoft 365 will fall into Microsoft's Baseline Protection, Sensitive Protection, or Highly Confidential Protection tiers. Most organizations will do well with **Baseline Protection**, which includes standard permissions barriers and basic security configurations. **Sensitive Protection** is useful for organizations that need to more strictly secure a subset of data in their environments, and it's probably useful for users who are accessing that sensitive data at an elevated level. **Highly Confidential Protection** is a small customer base that requires advanced protection options including encryption, Bring-Your-Own-Key (BYOK) scenarios, disabled external sharing, and more. You can find documentation and more info on each of the tiers at *https://docs.microsoft.com/en-us/office365/enterprise/microsoft-cloud-it-architecture-resources#identity-and-device-protection-for-office-365*.

In the following sub-sections, we cover specific data access topics in SharePoint, Teams, and Yammer.

SharePoint data access

Typically, the SharePoint Administrator role is granted to those who will be responsible for overseeing and managing the day-to-day operation and development of SharePoint site collections and the data governance they require.

Based on the protection tier your organization is aspiring to operate within, your SharePoint sites can be more or less restrictive than those from other organizations, or you might even use a combination of tier characteristics for different tenants or collections. For example:

- **Baseline.** This tier is for public and private team sites with external sharing enabled. Internal sharing is permitted, including site membership.

- **Sensitive.** This tier is only for private team sites that use warnings when sharing content externally. Internal sharing is permitted, but site membership other than built-in access requests are not permitted.

- **Highly Confidential.** This tier is only for private team sites with external sharing disabled/blocked and that has its files encrypted. Internal sharing is restricted, and access requests are disabled.

Your organization-wide sharing settings for SharePoint also apply to OneDrive. Any settings made at the tenant level cannot be overwritten to be less restrictive at individual site levels, but they could be made *more* restrictive should the owner want to do that. Microsoft suggests leaving the default sharing policy in place, which allows all sharing, including anonymous. Outlook and SharePoint will work together to give you better control over shares, as opposed to users circumventing security configurations and sharing in less-secure ways. You can set anonymous links to have an expiration date, and you can adjust the default share link type to be internal only so that external shares are only done intentionally.

As for device access, you can restrict unmanaged devices from certain activities in SharePoint, including downloading, syncing, and printing files. This can be done through the SharePoint admin center; choose **Policies** > **Access Control** > **Unmanaged Devices**. From here, your options are **Allow Full Access From Desk Apps, Mobile Apps, And The Web**; **Allow Limited, Web-Only Access**; and **Block Access**. (See Figure 3-2.)

Consider publishing retention for users to use in SharePoint as well. These labels can be applied to whole document libraries. Also, these labels can be applied individually to documents by their owners, or you can have labels automatically apply based on criteria you specify. Retention labels can be used in data loss prevention (DLP) policies, too. You can read specific steps in using retention policies and DLP in SharePoint at *https://docs.microsoft.com/en-us/microsoft-365/compliance/protect-sharepoint-online-files-with-office-365-labels-and-dlp*.

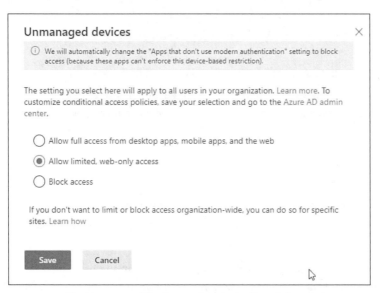

FIGURE 3-2 The Unmanaged Devices settings in the SharePoint admin center

Teams data access

Teams works together with other Office 365 apps and services so that the data that is being accessed in Teams is already protected by other security configurations. For example, Teams documents are stored in SharePoint document libraries and will be subject to any policies and configurations in place on that site.

Because Teams' content is spread across other apps, conditional access policies might not work as expected. This means a user can still access a SharePoint file directly or can access an Exchange calendar that's associated to the Team's group, even if a conditional access policy prevents Teams sign-ins. Because users can go directly to content without signing in to Teams through which to view it, they won't be restricted as intended.

Yammer data access

Yammer allows administrators to restrict data access to internal users only or even to those accessing via VPN (like SharePoint) or directly through the company network.

Also, you can create a Yammer-specific password policy if you are handling Yammer authentication separately from Office 365, or you can opt to manage identity through Office 365 so that users won't have multiple passwords and accounts. You can read more about enforcing Office 365 identity in Yammer at *https://docs.microsoft.com/en-us/Yammer/configure-your-yammer-network/enforce-office-365-identity*.

Configure B2B sharing for external users

Business-to-business (B2B) collaboration in Azure AD is what can allow users from other organizations (with Azure AD accounts) to securely access your apps and services. If a user doesn't have an Azure AD account, he or she can sign up for an account as an individual at *https://aka. ms/aip-signup,* or an account will be created when the user accepts a sharing invitation.

> **IMPORTANT   FUTURE OF B2B INVITATION REDEMPTION WITH ACCOUNT CREATION**
>
> Starting March 31, 2020, accounts are not automatically created for non-Azure AD users when an invite is accepted. Instead, Microsoft recommends emailing one-time passcodes for authentication.

As an administrator, you can:

- Disable external invitations
- Restrict invitations to admins and users with the Guest Inviter role
- Restrict invitations to admins, users with the Guest Inviter role, and current members
- Allow all users, including guests, to invite others (default)

To make your choice, go to the Azure portal (*https://portal.azure.com*) and navigate to **Azure Active Directory** > **External Identities** > **External Collaboration Settings**. You can configure the options there to create the appropriate restrictions and allowances for your organization. In Figure 3-3, the following settings have been enabled: **Guest Users Permissions Are Limited**; **Admins And Users In The Guest Inviter Role Can Invite**; **Members Can Invite**; and **Guests Can Invite**. The **Collaboration Restrictions** option has been set to **Allow Invitations To Be Sent To Any Domain (Most Inclusive)**.

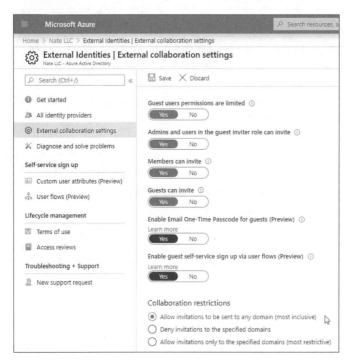

FIGURE 3-3   The External Collaboration Settings in Azure AD

Skill 3.2: Manage Azure Information Protection (AIP)

Azure Information Protection (AIP) is Microsoft's cloud solution that allows content encryption, device client deployment, policy implementation, automation of Sensitivity Label application, and more. In this skill, we'll cover AIP labels, policies, tenant keys, and integration with Office 365 Services.

> **This skill covers how to:**
> - Plan an AIP solution
> - Configure Sensitivity Labels and policies
> - Deploy the RMS connector
> - Manage tenant keys
> - Deploy the AIP client
> - Integrate AIP with Office 365 Services

Plan an AIP solution

AIP Sensitivity Labels are useful in helping to make sure proper safeguards and policies are applied to content when appropriate. Sensitivity Labels can be applied to content either automatically by policy or manually by users. If the AIP client is deployed to devices in your company, users can also get the added benefit of in-app-context recommendations via tooltips for an appropriate Sensitivity Label to apply.

For example, a document being created in the Microsoft Word desktop application containing credit card numbers might provide a tooltip upon recognition suggesting the document be labeled Highly Sensitive or PCI (Payment Card Industry). This makes it easy to be compliant and monitor organizational compliance with these kinds of sensitive data types. Something as simple as applying a label can automate the proper handling and access for specific data types.

Users know their own content best, and when properly trained to do so, they will do a good job of classifying their own content when appropriate. We use automation to catch the documents and content that fall through the cracks. We can create policies that search for known sensitive data types, such as Social Security and driver's license numbers, and then label the document accordingly.

To begin using AIP, you'll need to make sure you've already set up users and groups in Azure AD so that you can use them in policies and permissions. You'll also need to have licenses available to assign to all users who will be using AIP labels to classify their data.

Creating the AIP solution then entails configuring Sensitivity Labels and policies and deploying AIP clients, which we'll cover in this skill.

You might also want to install the AIPService PowerShell module for administration options by PowerShell. Formerly, the AIPService PowerShell module was called AADRM. If you still have AADRM, you'll need to remove it and install AIPService instead.

Configure Sensitivity Labels and policies

AIP includes several labels ready to use out-of-the-box. These can be customized or replaced as you see fit. The default labels are found in the AIP portal (*https://portal.azure.com*). Once there, search for **Azure Information Protection** and select it when it appears. Finally, click **Labels** to see the default labels available, including:

- **Personal.** Non-business data that is not typically important to more than a single user.
- **Public.** Business data intended for public consumption.
- **General.** Not intended for public consumption but may be shared with partners or specific external collaborators. Might include organization charts, directories, procedures, or internal communication.
- **Confidential.** Business data that could harm the business if shared outside appropriate parties, such as contracts, forecasts, sales data, and so on.
- **Highly Confidential.** Very sensitive information including passwords, personnel data, code, and client data.

From a user experience standpoint, you'll want to limit the number of additional labels you create and deploy in the organization. Also, you'll want to use easily understood company terminology to ensure the best chance of successful adoption and understanding. If the labels are intuitive, you have a better chance of ensuring that content will be better protected because classifying it appropriately was easy for your users.

Notice in Figure 3-4 how labels can be used in Policy, Marking (for purposes such as reporting), and Protection. The following default labels are available: Personal, Public, General, Confidential, and Highly Confidential. Confidential and Highly Confidential have sublabels for Recipients Only, All Employees, and Anyone (Not Protected).

Labels each have the following configuration options:

- **Policy.** Will show the name of the policy (if any) in which the label is deployed to users and groups. A label can only be used in one policy at a time.
- **Marking.** Will have visual indicators as users work with the content, such as headers or footers.
- **Protection.** Includes some specified method of protecting content, such as **Do Not Forward** automatically applied for emails. Normally a user would have to manually choose Do Not Forward from a new message's **Options** > **Encrypt** ribbon menu option. Automating this conditionally when paired with a label takes the guesswork out of when it's appropriate and makes sure you're protecting specific data types whether a user knows to or not.

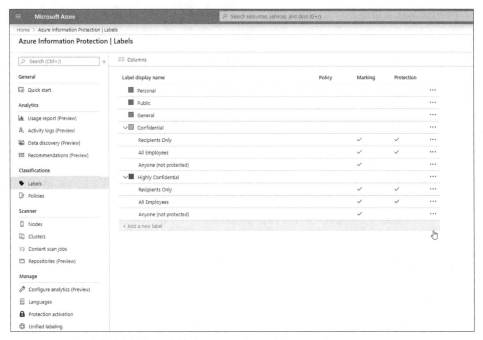

FIGURE 3-4   The default labels available in Azure Information Protection

To create a custom label beyond the default options, such as for protecting data related to a specific project, go to the AIP portal at *https://portal.azure.com* and search for **Azure Information Protection**. Once Azure Information Protection appears, click it and select **Labels** > **Add A New Label**. You then must configure the following settings for your custom label:

- **Enabled** (**On** or **Off**). You can leave the label **Off** until you're ready to activate it at a later time, or you can temporarily enable a custom label.
- **Name** and **Description.**
- **Color.** Use the default options or use custom colors by HEX code.
- **Protection.**
- **Not Configured.** Do nothing additional.
- **Protect.** Add protection from the following options:
    i. **Azure (Cloud Key)**
        1. **Set Permissions.** Add users.
        2. **Set User-Defined Permissions.** Apply Do Not Forward and/or prompt user for permissions.
        3. Select a predefined template.

ii. **HYOK (AD RMS)**

- **Remove Protection.** Remove any existing protection.
- **Visual Marking.** Configure formatting and appearance for any labels added to content.
  - **Header.** Add a header to documents with this label.
  - **Footer.** Add a footer to documents with this label.
  - **Watermark.** Watermark documents with this label.
- **Conditions.** For automatic application or recommendation.
  - Standard sensitive information types (such as license or passport numbers, credit card numbers, and so on).
  - **Custom Phrase** or **Regular Expression.**
- **Application Automatic** or **Recommended**.
- **Policy Tip Customization.** Use for explaining Automatic or Recommended labels.

Policies are also created in the AIP portal at *https://portal.azure.com.* Search for **Azure Information Protection**, and once Azure Information Protection appears, click it and then choose **Policies** > **Add A New Policy**. New policies have the following settings you can configure:

- Name and description.
- Users and email-enabled groups to whom the policy applies (who can use the label).
- Label(s) to include/publish in the policy for selected users.
- Default label, which is a label to provide as a default option for users to whom this policy applies.
- Send logging data to Azure Information Protection analytics. See what sort of data is made available on this dashboard at *https://docs.microsoft.com/en-us/azure/informa-tion-protection/reports-aip.*
- All documents and emails must have a label (**On** or **Off**).
- Users must provide justification to remove or lessen a label (**On** or **Off**).
- For emails, apply label of attachment with the highest classification to the email itself (**Off**, **Automatic**, or **Recommended**).
- Display the Information Protection Bar in Office Apps (**On** or **Off**).
- Add the Do Not Forward Button to Outlook (**On** or **Off**).

- Make the custom permissions options available to users (**On** or **Off**).
- Optional URL for **Tell Me More** link for user tips and info when working with AIP.

Once created, both policies and labels can be rearranged to alter the order in which they appear and/or apply for users.

Deploy the RMS connector

Azure Rights Management Service (Azure RMS) is a cloud-based solution capable of working with the on-premises IRM functionality by deploying an RMS connector. RMS connectors can be installed on virtual machines or physical, on-premises servers if they're running Windows 2008 R2 or later. For example, you could install it on Exchange or SharePoint servers if you like, though you would want to install it on at least two machines for high availability. Follow these steps to deploy an RMS connector:

1. Download and install the RMS connector (available at *https://go.microsoft.com/fwlink/?LinkId=314106*).

2. Enter your credentials.

3. Authorize servers you'll configure in step 5 that may use the RMS connector.

4. Configure load balancing and the high availability of the connector across at least two servers.

5. Configure servers (such as Exchange, SharePoint, and File Resource Manager servers) that will use the RMS connector.

Manage tenant keys

A tenant key is like an umbrella encompassing these subkeys:

- User keys
- Computer keys
- Document encryption keys

By default, Microsoft automatically generates and manages your tenant key. This default arrangement is the most cost-effective and fastest method of getting started with utilizing AIP. It requires minimal administrative effort and is often the best option for smaller organizations.

Some organizations, especially those with strict compliance requirements, might be required to manage their own tenant keys via Bring-Your-Own-Key (BYOK). BYOK keys can be created in the Azure Key Vault or an on-premises HSM, which requires Azure Key Vault Premium where the key would be imported.

Deploy the AIP client

There are two AIP clients that can be deployed in your environment:

- Azure Information Protection client (classic)
- Azure Information Protection unified labeling client

The classic AIP client downloads labels and information from Azure. The unified labeling client is the more recent and recommended option that combines labels and information from each of the following locations:

- Microsoft 365 Security Center (*https://security.microsoft.com*)
- Microsoft 365 Compliance Center (*https://compliance.microsoft.com*)
- Office 365 Security & Compliance Center (*https://protection.office.com*)

By deploying AIP clients to machines in your organization, you're essentially expanding coverage of the AIP solution and more conveniently providing protection and guidance to users on their machines and in-context in applications when working. This increases the likelihood that users will effectively adopt labeling and data classification as part of their collaboration routines. AIP clients on machines enable in-product label recommendations, such as tooltips and headers in Outlook, Word, and so on, which appear as users create and work with content.

The classic client might be the preferred pick if you require advanced features such as Hold-Your-Own-Key (HYOK) on-premises or if your labels have yet to be migrated to the unified labeling client.

Generally, the unified labeling client would be a good choice ensuring you'd be receiving product updates going forward. It also supports macOS, iOS, and Android devices while the classic client doesn't.

Integrate AIP with Office 365 Services

AIP for Office 365 is included in Office 365 E3 and E5 licenses. An additional AIP P1 or P2 license is required to use classification and labeling. AIP integrates with Exchange Online (automatically enabled in new tenants), SharePoint, and OneDrive for Business.

To configure SharePoint and OneDrive IRM (because they're not automatic like Exchange), a global or SharePoint administrator will need to go to the SharePoint admin center and then choose **Settings** > **Classic Settings Page**. Scroll down and select **Use The IRM Service Specified In Your Configuration**. Finally, choose **Refresh IRM Settings**, as shown in Figure 3-5.

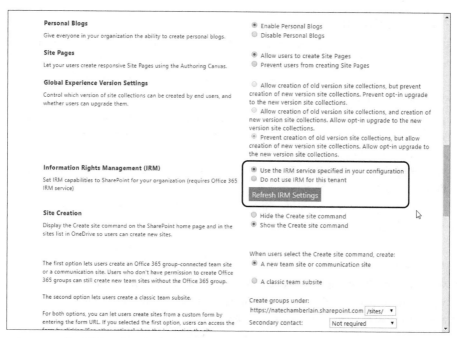

FIGURE 3-5 The IRM settings for both SharePoint and OneDrive found in the SharePoint admin center

Skill 3.3: Manage Data Loss Prevention (DLP)

Data Loss Prevention (DLP) in Office 365 makes it easier for organizations to adhere to compliance regulations and protect data and users by monitoring the movement of sensitive data within and outside of the company. This skill will focus on planning a DLP solution, working with DLP policies, using sensitive information types, and monitoring DLP topics of interest.

> **This skill covers how to:**
> - Plan a DLP solution
> - Create and manage DLP policies
> - Create and manage sensitive information types
> - Monitor DLP reports
> - Manage DLP notifications

Plan a DLP solution

Your DLP solution will include a combination of DLP policies you configure, as well as custom and standard sensitive information types you integrate with those policies. Those policies are capable of monitoring and reporting on specific activities and data in your organization and/or taking action based on that monitoring.

Multiple policies can be assigned to the same users and groups, and these policies might overlap in detection of certain data types. For example, you can have a policy that will detect HIPAA-protected data and a separate policy that also detects PII identifiers (which is included in the default HIPAA policy template). This means multiple actions could be taken for the same activity, depending on policy configuration.

In the following sections, we cover the configuration of policies, sensitive information types, reports, and notifications to help build a comprehensive DLP solution in your organization.

EXAM TIP **DLP SCOPE**

Yammer groups and Power Apps cannot be protected by a DLP policy. However, the content you may encounter or manipulate in a Power App (such as data from a SharePoint list) can be protected, as can content that is shared as links or attachments in Yammer.

Create and manage DLP policies

DLP policies are what power the active monitoring of your environment for potential data loss. Through these policies, you decide what to watch for and how to respond to risky or dangerous data movement.

DLP policies can include and/or exclude locations in

- Exchange email
- SharePoint sites
- OneDrive accounts
- Teams chat and channel messages

DLP policies typically contain

- Locations to which the policy applies (SharePoint, Exchange, and the like)
- Rules (including conditions and actions)

To create a new DLP policy, go to the Office 365 Security & Compliance Center at *https://protection.office.com,* and choose **Data Loss Prevention** > **Policy** > **Create A Policy**.

First, you'll select a template using predefined **Financial**, **Medical And Health**, or **Privacy** data types, or you can choose to create a **Custom** policy with the data types selected and combined a la carte. If you've created custom sensitive information types, chances are you'd be creating a custom policy to utilize it. See Figure 3-6 for the DLP policy wizard's Choose The

Information To Protect screen in which you select a template. For demonstration, we'll proceed with creating a HIPAA policy.

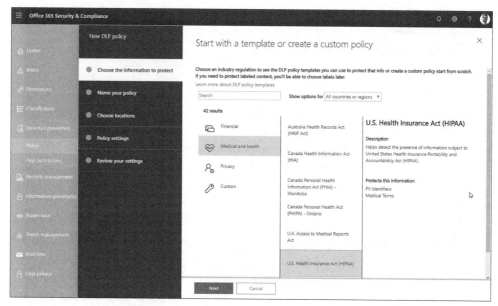

FIGURE 3-6 Creating a new DLP policy and choosing a template

1. Once a template has been selected, click **Next**.

2. Name and describe the policy and click **Next**.

3. Choose locations in which you'd like to protect content with this policy. Your options are:
   - **Protect Content In Exchange Email, Teams Chats And Channel Messages And OneDrive And SharePoint Documents.**
   - **Let Me Choose Specific Locations.** Customize which locations and sublocations, such as specific sites to include or exclude from the policy.

4. Click **Next**.

5. Customize the content types to include. In this step, you'll see the data types pre-selected with the template you chose. Click **Next**.
   - If you chose a template, you can edit the pre-selected data types and you can choose whether to detect when content is shared outside or only within the organization.
   - Alternatively, you can choose to ignore the pre-selected data types at this point and choose **Use Advanced Settings** instead.

6. Choose actions to take when sensitive info is detected. Click **Next**.
   - You can enable policy tips, which warn and educate users when content will be protected by the DLP policy.
   - Choose whether to send incident reports via email to specific recipients.
   - You can also restrict access to or encrypt the detected content.

7. Choose a start option from the following:

   - **Yes, Turn It On Right Away**
   - **I'd Like To Test It Out First** (with an additional option to **Show Policy Tips While In Test Mode**)
   - **No, Keep It Off. I'll Turn It On Later**

8. Click **Next**.

9. Review the policy settings and click **Create**.

All the DLP policies you've created will appear in the **Data Loss Prevention** > **Policy** node of the Office 365 Security & Compliance Center. Each will be listed with its current status (**On**, **Off**, or **Testing**) and can be reordered to change the manner in which they're applied if more than one applies to specific content.

The top of this page (**Policy** node) also shows two graphic representations of DLP policy matches over time and false positives and overrides over time.

REAL WORLD **DLP POLICIES**

Industry-specific compliance requirements, such as HIPAA in the healthcare industry, help in creating these policies by defining the data types required to be protected or handled in a specific way within your organization. For example, Microsoft has already "bundled" the sensitive information types that HIPAA protects. When creating your custom DLP policy, you can simply start from the **Medical and Health** > **U.S. Health Insurance Act (HIPAA)** template. From there, you can keep it as-is out-of-the-box, or you can make adjustments to fine-tune it for your organization.

Create and manage sensitive information types

DLP policies you create can include checks for sensitive information types you create. For example, you might add a sensitive information type for a specific confidential project in your organization.

Default sensitive information types that are already available for usage (such as credit card numbers, Social Security numbers, license numbers, and so on) aren't just numeric patterns but are identified using a combination of keywords, internal functions, evaluation of regular expressions (regex), and other content examination to guarantee the highest likelihood of a match and to reduce false positives.

To create a new, custom DLP sensitive information type, open the Office 365 Security & Compliance Center at *https://protection.office.com*, and choose **Classification** > **Sensitive Info Types** > **Create**.

1. Name and describe the sensitive info type. Click **Next**.

2. Click **Add Element**. Add elements you'd like to include in the definition of the sensitive info type. You'll choose matching content (primary element) and optional supporting elements. For each sensitive information type, you'll configure the following options:

   - **Matching Element.** From one or a combination of the following content match options, define the primary identifying characteristics of the sensitive information type being created:

     i. **Detect Content Containing**

        1. **Keywords**

        2. **Regular Expression**

        3. **Dictionary (Large Keywords)**

   - **Supporting Elements.** This is optional and is used to increase the accuracy of matches and reduce false positives. Choose from or combine the following options to define supporting elements for this sensitive information type:

     ii. **Contains This Regular Expression**

     iii. **Contains This Keyword List**

     iv. **Contains This Dictionary (Large Keywords)**

   - **Confidence Level.** Use this setting to match the confidence percentage of the pattern.

   - **Character Proximity.** This sets the proximity of the supporting elements to the primary matching content.

3. Click **Next**.

4. Review and then click **Finish**.

Monitor DLP reports

There are three DLP reports in the Office 365 Security & Compliance Center that you can utilize to monitor DLP policy performance:

- **DLP Policy Matches.** Instances when a DLP policy found specified data and executed a policy's actions. This report focuses on rule match counts.

- **DLP False Positives And Overrides.** Instances in which detections were reported false or users chose to override policy actions.

- **DLP Incidents.** Like the DLP policy match report, this focuses on DLP policy executions, but it reports content match counts as opposed to rule matches.

To access these reports, go to the Office 365 Security & Compliance Center at *https://protection.office.com*, choose **Reports** > **Dashboard**, and look for the cards for each of the reports listed. You can select any of the report cards to view a larger, more-detailed version of the chart.

Manage DLP notifications

DLP notifications include both email notifications as well as policy tips that appear as users are working in-context on content that a DLP policy will apply to.

Emails are straightforward and can be sent to specific people or to the people who last worked on the content.

Policy tips present themselves when a user is working in a document that contains sensitive information that is protected by a policy. For example, if a user is editing a list of customers and their Social Security numbers, they'll see a yellow banner across the top of the relevant Office app, which lets them know a message/tip you've written for that particular policy's notification.

Configuration of both DLP notification options is done as part of the policy configuration. To get started, go to the Office 365 Security & Compliance Center at *https://protection.office.com* and choose **Data Loss Prevention** > **Policy**. Lastly, either choose an existing policy or create a new one.

When you get to the policy settings screen, you'll find an area for user notifications. Figure 3.7 shows where you configure the type and content of notifications.

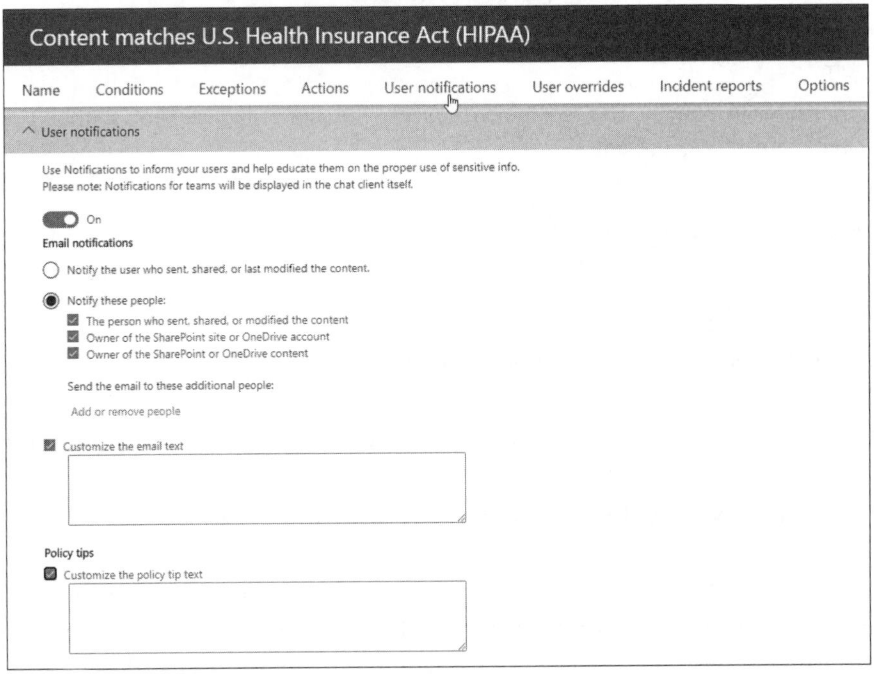

FIGURE 3-7 The user notifications screen of a DLP policy

Skill 3.4: Implement and manage Microsoft Cloud App Security

Cloud App Security (CAS) allows administrators to monitor and manage connected cloud apps (such as G Suite), lessen the likelihood of data loss by tracking anomalous activity, and deploy conditional access policies that restrict access to these third-party organization apps (similar to how you've already configured Office 365 conditional access policies).

> **This skill covers how to:**
> - Plan Cloud App Security implementation
> - Configure Microsoft Cloud App Security
> - Manage cloud app discovery
> - Manage entries in the Cloud app catalog
> - Manage apps in Cloud App Security
> - Manage Microsoft Cloud App Security
> - Configure Cloud App Security connectors and OAuth apps
> - Configure Cloud App Security policies and templates
> - Review, interpret, and respond to Cloud App Security alerts, reports, dashboards, and logs

Plan Cloud App Security implementation

Microsoft Cloud App Security (CAS) is included with the Microsoft 365 E5 subscription bundles, the Enterprise Mobility + Security E5 subscription, or as a standalone add-on; CAS is licensed per-user.

It's important to note that Microsoft Cloud App Security (with more than 16,000 apps) is not the same as Office 365 Cloud App Security (with only about 750 apps). Microsoft CAS *includes* Office 365 CAS and does not require an Office 365 subscription. Office 365 CAS is specific to Office 365 environments and is a subset of Microsoft CAS.

Once an adequate subscription including Microsoft CAS exists, a Global Administrator or Security Administrator can configure Microsoft Cloud App Security.

Configure Microsoft Cloud App Security

To begin setting up Microsoft CAS, go to the CAS portal at *https://portal.cloudappsecurity.com* and then click the settings gear from the upper-right corner and select **Settings**.

As seen in Figure 3-8, this is where you'll configure your organization details such as **Organization Display Name** (appears on webpages and emails to employees); **Environment**

Name (helps differentiate when you have multiple environments in the same organization); your logo; and the domains you manage.

The domains you choose to list in **Managed Domains** are important for determining who appears as an external user in reports. Because external user activity isn't monitored like your internal users, you'll want to be sure all domains you manage are included for the most accurate insight into your CAS environment.

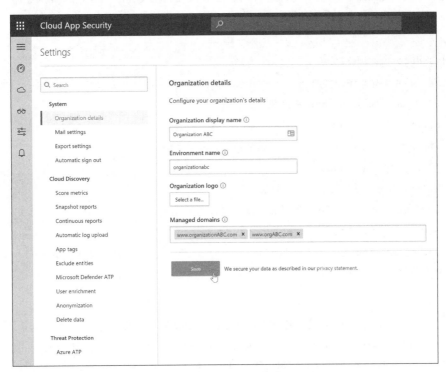

FIGURE 3-8 The Organization details screen of Microsoft CAS settings

Lastly, check out the official network requirements documentation at *https://docs.microsoft.com/en-us/cloud-app-security/network-requirements* for IP addresses and DNS names you'll need to whitelist based on your environment.

Manage cloud app discovery

Cloud discovery enables you to have a window through which to monitor data flow outside your organization. Within cloud app discovery, you can create two types of reports:

- **Snapshot.** These reports are generated from manually uploaded logs.
- **Continuous.** These use machine learning to analyze continuous network log uploads or connections for anomalous activity.

To create a snapshot report, go to the Microsoft CAS portal and choose **Discover** > **Create Snapshot Report**.

To configure continuous reports, go to the settings gear in the upper-right corner and select **Log Collectors.** From there, you can configure the data sources and/or log collectors that will serve as the continuous source of traffic data to be analyzed.

Manage entries in the Cloud app catalog

To add a custom app to the Cloud app catalog, first go to the Cloud Discovery Dashboard by opening the Microsoft CAS portal and choosing **Discover** > **Cloud Discovery Dashboard** from the left-hand navigation menu.

To add custom apps, follow these instructions:

1. Click the three dots (ellipsis) in the upper-right corner and select **Add New Custom App**.

2. Add the details for the app including:

   - **Name** and **Description**
   - **Category**
   - **Domains** (unique domains used to access this app)
   - **IPv4 Addresses** and/or **IPv6 Addresses**
   - **Hosting Platform** (such as Azure)
   - **Business Unit** (optional)
   - **Score** (risk score)

3. Click **Create**.

To manage existing entries, simply search the Cloud App catalog for the apps you want to manage. See the next section for more details.

Manage apps in Cloud App Security

Once you've connected to apps in Cloud App Security, you can manage them (and connect to additional apps) by going to the CAS portal and choosing **Investigate** > **Connected Apps**.

Depending on the app, you might have different options for each app, such as editing the instance name, the connection properties, and so on. The options are chosen by clicking the three dots (ellipsis) menu that appears to the right of the app's name.

If you select a connected app, you'll be able to see data such as:

- Status
- Connection date/time
- Last health check date/time
- Who connected the app
- Protected accounts
- Last activity log

- Last DLP scan file count
- Real-time scan status

Manage Microsoft Cloud App Security

Cloud App Security involves policies that allow you to better manage user activity and behavior in the cloud as well as respond to risks and threats.

CAS policies can be of the following types:

- **Access Policy.** Real-time user login monitoring and reporting.
- **Activity Policy.** Monitor and enforce policies via provider APIs.
- **Anomaly Detection Policy.** Find unusual activity in your organization for an app or user.
- **App Discovery Policy.** Be alerted when new apps are detected in your environment.
- **Cloud Discovery Anomaly Detection Policy.** Unusual activity for a user or app detected in Cloud Discovery app logs.
- **File Policy.** Find specific data types and apply governance actions.
- **Session Policy.** Real-time monitoring and control over user activity, such as printing or downloading from web apps.

Your CAS management will employ policies like these to watch for security vulnerabilities in threats related to:

- Privileged identities
- Sharing control
- DLP
- Cloud discovery
- Compliance
- Configuration control (unauthorized changes)

With policies like these adjusted to suit your needs and environment, you're able to automatically respond to and reduce risk in your organization as users work across multiple apps to execute routine business processes.

Configure Cloud App Security connectors and OAuth apps

To configure connectors, go to the CAS portal and choose **Investigate** > **Connected Apps** (to connect directly to apps like Office 365, G Suite, Dropbox, and so on) or **OAuth apps** (to monitor OAuth requests for access to your environment).

To add a new connector, choose **Connected Apps**, click the + (plus sign), and then click the app to which you'd like to connect CAS (such as Office 365 or Dropbox). Each connector/app will request different information to authenticate to the app and securely utilize its APIs.

Because Office 365 is likely to be a common connector being added in many organizations, the specific steps for making that connection are as follows:

1. Go to the CAS portal and choose **Investigate** > **Connected Apps**. Then click the **+** (plus sign) and choose **Office 365**.

2. Choose which components to monitor:

   - Azure AD Users And Groups
   - Azure AD Management Events
   - Azure AD Sign-In Events
   - Azure AD Apps
   - Office 365 Activities
   - Office 365 Files (requires enabling file monitoring by choosing **Settings** > **Files**)

3. Click **Connect**.

To add a new OAuth app, choose **OAuth apps** > **New Policy From Search**. For each OAuth policy, configure the following settings:

- **Policy Name.**
- **Description.**
- **Policy Severity.** Choose **Low**, **Medium**, or **High**.
- **Category.** Choose from the following options:
  - **Access Control**
  - **Cloud Discovery**
  - **Compliance**
  - **Configuration Control**
  - **DLP**
  - **Privileged Accounts**
  - **Sharing Control**
  - **Threat Detection**
- **App To Which It Applies.** Such as Office 365 for when third-party calendar apps might request Office 365 calendar access.
- **Filters.** Such as permission level requested and community use pattern.
- **Alerts.** Send the alert as an email, text message, or send to Power Automate to be used in a flow.

Configure Cloud App Security policies and templates

You can create policies from scratch or from templates, which is similar to how we created DLP policies. To do either, go to the CAS portal, choose **Control**, and select either **Policies** (to create from scratch) or **Templates** (to use a template).

To create a new policy:

1. Go to the CAS portal and choose **Control** > **Policies** > **Create Policy**.

2. Select the type of policy to create:

   - **Access Policy.** (Monitor login activity across cloud apps.)

   - **Activity Policy.** (Monitor specific activities performed by users or large volumes of the same activity such as bulk downloads.)

   - **App Discovery Policy.** (Receive a notification when new apps are found in your company.)

   - **Cloud Discovery Anomaly Detection Policy.** (Configure risk factors and then get alerts for abnormal activity.)

   - **File Policy.** (Apply governance actions based on scans of cloud apps for risky sharing activity or the presence of sensitive data.)

   - **OAuth App Policy.** (Get notifications when OAuth apps meet specific criteria such as when apps require a high permission level and have been authorized by more than a specific number of users.)

   - **Session Policy.** (Monitor and respond to user activity in real-time.)

3. Based on the policy you're creating, you'll have different fields to configure. Make selections for the template, severity, category, filters, alerts/notifications, and governance actions where appropriate, and then click **Create**. See Figure 3-9 for an idea of some of the fields for configuration when creating an Activity policy.

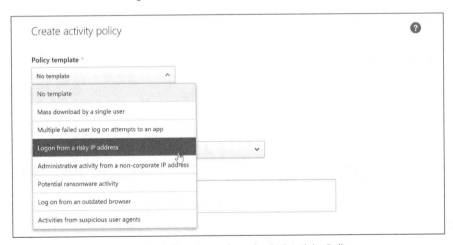

FIGURE 3-9 The Policy Template being chosen from the CAS Activity Policy

To create a policy from a template:

1. Go to the CAS portal, select **Control** > **Templates** and choose the plus sign (**+**) next to the template you'd like to use. These include templates such as the following:

   - **File Shared With Unauthorized Domain**
   - **Mass Download By A Single User**
   - **Multiple Failed User Log On Attempts To An App**
   - **New Popular App**
   - **New High-Volume App**

2. The policy will be partially created for you based on the selected template. Figure 3-10 shows a Cloud Discovery Anomaly Detection Policy created using a template.

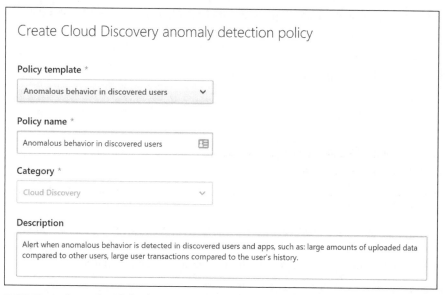

Create Cloud Discovery anomaly detection policy

Policy template *

Anomalous behavior in discovered users

Policy name *

Anomalous behavior in discovered users

Category *

Cloud Discovery

Description

Alert when anomalous behavior is detected in discovered users and apps, such as: large amounts of uploaded data compared to other users, large user transactions compared to the user's history.

FIGURE 3-10 Anomalous Behavior In Discovered Users chosen from the Policy Template drop-down menu

To monitor your policies, go to the CAS Portal and choose **Control** > **Policies**. From there, you can filter policies by the same characteristics we covered in creation of CAS policies:

- **Name (Search).** Name of the policy you'd like to review.
- **Type.** Drop-down menu to choose the type of policy to filter to, such as **Access Policy**, **Activity Policy**, **Anomaly Detection**, and the like.
- **Status.** Choose **Active** or **Disabled**.
- **Severity.** Choose **Low**, **Medium**, or **High**.
- **Risk Category.** The type of risk the policy helps reduce, such as **Access Control**, **Cloud Discovery**, **Compliance**, **DLP**, and so on.

For each listed policy, there is a vertical ellipsis (three dots) menu, from which you have several options per policy. By clicking the ellipsis, you can **Edit Policy**, **View All Matches**, **View All Alerts**, **Disable**, or **Delete**. The ellipses appearing after the Disable and Delete options are there to signify that you'll be asked to confirm your choice before it's final. This is helpful in case you accidentally select one of these options (or choose the wrong option).

By monitoring matches and alerts, you'll be better able to fine-tune policies to catch helpful and relevant information and find fewer false positives. You might also discover the need for additional policies based on user behavior or activity trends.

Review, interpret, and respond to Cloud App Security alerts, reports, dashboards, and logs

There are several ways to analyze and respond to data from Cloud App Security. In this skill, we'll cover the review, interpretation, and response options for each of them, including:

- CAS alerts
- CAS dashboards and reports
- CAS logs

CAS alerts

Before you will receive CAS alerts, you must have policies that are set up to create alerts as part of their risk mitigation and response.

Once you have policies creating CAS alerts, they can be accessed by choosing **Alerts** from the CAS portal.

In the policy itself, you can choose to also send alerts by email, text message, and Power Automate. The CAS portal then serves as a dashboard for reporting and analysis while your immediate alert notifications are sent via your preferred method to relevant parties.

For alerts on the dashboard, you can do the following:

- **Dismiss** the alert if it is irrelevant or a non-issue. When you **Dismiss** alerts, you have the option to provide a **Comment** about why you're dismissing it (for internal tracking) and/or **Send Us Feedback About This Alert** to help Microsoft improve matches in the future.
- **Resolve**.
- Mark as unread to handle later.
- Adjust the policy to improve future matches.
- Optionally, you can enter a resolution comment and/or alert match feedback.

CAS dashboards and reports

There are three data management reports to help in analyzing your environment. You can view and export these reports from the CAS by choosing **Investigate** > **Files** node:

- **Data Sharing Overview.** All files stored in all apps.
- **Outbound Sharing By Domain.** Domains to which files are shared.
- **Owners Of Shared Files.** Owners of externally shared files.

To access these reports, go to the CAS portal, click **Investigate**, choose the **Files** node, and select the three dots (ellipsis) menu from the upper-right corner.

Based on the data in these reports, you may choose to design new policies or adjust existing policies to mitigate identified risks.

CAS logs

The CAS log might be useful if you need to determine or review which users modified files in another user's OneDrive or which users downloaded files from a SharePoint site. While these are very specific examples, the CAS logs can encompass all sorts of activities (both simple and complex) across all apps to which you've connected CAS.

To access the CAS logs, choose **Investigate** > **Activity Log**, and then use the filters to drill down to the data you're interested in analyzing. You can filter the CAS activity log using the following filters:

- **Queries.** You can choose **Admin Activities**, **Download Activities**, **Failed Log In**, **File and Folder Activities**, and the like.
- **App.** You can restrict the log to items including activities only in specific apps, such as Microsoft CAS, Office 365, SharePoint, Exchange, and so on.
- **User Name.** You can filter and find activities from specific users involved in the activity that is logged.
- **Raw IP Address.** This text field allows you to limit the log to specific IP addresses from where the activity took place.
- **Activity Type.** You can filter countless activities including or involving access requests, policy activities, downloads, content changes, views, and the like.
- **Location.** You can filter the CAS log to a specific country of access.

Similar to the filters available along the top of the CAS log, you can review the list (filtered or not) with these fields available for review:

- **Activity.** Access requests, policy activity, downloads, content changes, views, and the like.
- **User.** User involved in the activity that was logged, or N/A if not applicable.
- **App.** Microsoft CAS, Office 365, SharePoint, Exchange, and so on.
- **IP Address.** IP address where the activity took place, also indicating whether the IP address is from a cloud provider.

- **Location.** Country of access and also indicates whether the location is a data center.

- **Device.** Device type, operating system, and browser used to perform the activity.

- **Date.** Date/time of the specific activity.

Thought Experiments

In the following Thought Experiments, apply what you've learned in this chapter. You can find answers to these questions in the "Thought Experiment Answers" section at the end of this chapter.

Secure data access within Office 365

1. You need a solution to meet a compliance requirement that states you must audit external access to your environment, including Microsoft support connections. What could you utilize?

   A. Microsoft Cloud App Security

   B. Customer Lockbox

   C. Microsoft Support requests

   D. Conditional access policies

2. A conditional access policy restricting access to Teams keeps unwanted viewers from accessing the Team's content stored in SharePoint as well.

   A. True

   B. False

3. Which of the following is not a possibility when configuring B2B external sharing?

   A. One-time passcodes for guest users

   B. Restricting sharing to specific domains

   C. Having external B2B users complete access reviews

   D. Allowing guests to invite other guests

Manage Azure Information Protection (AIP)

1. You create a label named *TopSecret* and include it in an Azure Information Protection (AIP) policy. A user uses the label to email sensitive content to external recipients. The external recipients can't open the content, however. You create a new label and have the original user resend the message using the different label. Could this solve the issue?

   A. Yes

   B. No

2. You create a label named *TopSecret* and include it in an Azure Information Protection (AIP) policy. A user uses the label to email sensitive content to external recipients. The external recipients can't open the content, however. You decide to modify the existing label settings. Could this solve the issue?

   A. Yes

   B. No

3. You want to empower users to reclassify emails or documents after they've already been automatically labeled by policy. Which solution would allow you to require that the user provide justification when lessening the protection of the content?

   A. AIP Policy

   B. Azure AD access review

   C. Conditional access policy

   D. DLP policy

Manage Data Loss Prevention (DLP)

1. You've already published retention labels to Exchange. What step is still needed to make them available to users to manually assign to their messages?

   A. Create a DLP policy making the labels available to specific users

   B. Grant the Security Administrator role to eligible users

   C. Create an AIP policy making the labels available to specific users

   D. Create a conditional access policy making the labels available to specific users

2. A manager complains that she's receiving DLP policy match emails too frequently and they're mostly false positives. What should you adjust to lessen the frequency?

   A. Modify the user override settings

   B. Modify the app scope of the policy

   C. Modify the matched activities threshold

   D. Modify the policy's policy tips

3. What is required to be configured before users can manually indicate content that needs to be protected by a DLP policy?

    A. AIP policies

    B. Custom sensitive information types

    C. Retention labels

    D. RMS connector deployment

Implement and manage Microsoft Cloud App Security

1. You need to determine which users accessed and modified files in another user's OneDrive. Which can you use?

    A. CAS activity log

    B. Azure AD audit log

    C. eDiscovery case

    D. DLP policy match history

2. Which type of CAS policy would allow you to block printing from SharePoint Online?

    A. Cloud Discovery Anomaly Detection

    B. Session

    C. Activity

    D. OAuth app

3. If you have a CAS file policy that's looking for content with the word "Mongoose" in the filename, which file would NOT be subject to the policy?

    A. MongooseFile.docx

    B. ProjectMngse.pdf

    C. Mongoose_Doc.xlsx

    D. Mongoose.pptx

Thought Experiment Answers

This section contains the solutions to the thought experiments and answers to the skill review questions in this chapter.

Secure data access within Office 365

1. B
2. B
3. C

Manage Azure Information Protection (AIP)

1. A
2. B
3. A

Manage Data Loss Prevention (DLP)

1. A
2. C
3. C

Implement and manage Microsoft Cloud App Security

1. A
2. B
3. B

CHAPTER 4

Manage governance and compliance features in Microsoft 365

The final domain covers governance and compliance within Office 365. While some larger organizations may have dedicated teams responsible for this, many others look to the information security team or the IT admins to address this—usually reactively. This chapter starts with reporting and auditing, which are critical security features that are vital for enforcing governance and ensuring compliance.

Skills in this chapter:

- Skill 4.1: Configure and analyze security reporting
- Skill 4.2: Manage and analyze audit logs and reports
- Skill 4.3: Configure Office 365 classification and labeling
- Skill 4.4: Manage data governance and retention
- Skill 4.5: Manage search and investigation
- Skill 4.6: Manage data privacy regulation compliance

Skill 4.1: Configure and analyze security reporting

This section focuses on the wealth of data that is available to Office 365 customers, including telemetry, reports, and alerts. You should focus on what information is available where, including which portals are used and the options that can be configured with each.

> **In this skill, you learn how to:**
> - Implement Windows Analytics
> - Configure Windows Telemetry options
> - Configure Office Telemetry options
> - Review and interpret security reports and dashboards
> - Plan for custom security reporting with Intelligent Security Graph
> - Review Office 365 Secure Score actions and recommendations
> - Configure alert policies in the Office 365 Security and Compliance Center

Interpret Windows Analytics

Windows Analytics provides administrators with rich insights into the devices that are in your environment. Originally, this data was intended to help admins plan for upgrades to Windows 10; however, Upgrade Readiness and Device Health solutions were both retired in early 2020. For the exam, you should be familiar with both because it can take time for exams to be updated to reflect the current state.

Device Health can be used to determine the following:

- Devices that frequently crash, which might indicate a need to be replaced
- Device drivers that cause crashes and might need to be upgraded or replaced
- Windows Information Protection misconfigurations that might affect the users' experience

Upgrade Readiness includes tools that enable admins to plan and execute upgrades from Windows 7 or Windows 8.1 to Windows 10. You can use Upgrade Readiness to get the following:

- Visual workflows for the upgrade process
- Detailed hardware and software inventory
- Search capabilities
- Application and driver compatibility information and recommendations
- Application usage information

You can export this data to use with System Center Configuration Manager and other software deployment tools.

Configure Windows Telemetry options

By default, Windows 10 shares diagnostic data with Microsoft, but some customers might prefer to restrict what data is shared or to prevent sharing entirely. Administrators can use either Group Policy or Mobile Device Management to centrally configure settings; local administrators can use registry keys on individual machines to do the same. There are four levels of diagnostic data that can be set, as shown in Table 4-1.

TABLE 4-1 Windows Telemetry options

Level	Value
Security	0
Basic	1
Enhanced	2
Full	3

Use the corresponding value in the policy setting to match the level of telemetry you want to permit:

1. In the Group Policy Management Console, browse to **Computer Configuration** > **Administrative Templates** > **Windows Components** > **Data Collection And Preview Builds**.

2. Double-click **Allow Telemetry** and set it to **Enabled**. (If you want to disable telemetry completely, you can do that here, too.)

3. Click **Options**, and then under **Value**, choose the desired level, as shown in Table 4-1.

> **NEED MORE REVIEW?**
>
> The data that is shared with each of the levels is documented at *https://docs.microsoft.com/ en-us/windows/privacy/configure-windows-diagnostic-data-in-your-organization*.

> **NOTE SETTINGS CORRESPOND TO THE OS**
>
> It's important to note that these settings only correspond to the operating system. In addition to Microsoft's telemetry settings, third-party applications might have their own telemetry settings, which need to be configured separately.

Configure Office Telemetry options

Microsoft Office collects telemetry separately from the operating system and might share data from your documents to enable connected experiences, such as translation, grammar checking, and other functions. You can configure the level of telemetry shared, and you can choose to disable data sharing. Note that disabling connected experiences might limit functionality your users desire.

> **NEED MORE REVIEW? MORE ABOUT PRIVACY CONTROLS**
>
> You can read more about the level of detail shared and the potential effects of disabling sharing at *https://docs.microsoft.com/en-us/deployoffice/privacy/overview-privacy-controls*.

Administrators can use Group Policy or the Office cloud policy service to manage settings for Office ProPlus or edit the registry directly. Users can access these settings directly by choosing **Options** > **Advanced** from within an Office application.

To manage settings for users using Group Policy, download the latest ADMX files from Microsoft and adjust settings by navigating to **User Configuration** > **Policies** > **Administrative Templates** > **Microsoft Office 2016** > **Privacy** >**Trust Center**. Specifics are documented at *https://docs.microsoft.com/en-us/deployoffice/privacy/manage-privacy-controls*.

Review and interpret security reports and dashboards

The Security Dashboard in the Office 365 Security & Compliance Center is one of the key places in which security admins will spend time in Office 365. This dashboard, which is the home page of the Office 365 Security & Compliance Center, includes security insights as well as reports about the top information admins need to know. It is also where admins can download reports and manage schedules for reports that need to be run regularly in their environments, and it includes recommendations admins should follow to help secure their environments. To access the Security Dashboard, you need to have one of the following roles: Global Administrator, Security Administrator, or Security Reader.

There are several widgets in the Security Dashboard. You can arrange them to suit your needs and pin those that are more important to you to the home page. Some of the more useful widgets are shown in Table 4-2.

Figure 4-1 shows the Top Insights & Recommendations widget.

TABLE 4-2 Security Dashboard reports

Widget	Description
Top Insights & Recommendations	This widget highlights things in your environment that can indicate malicious activities so that you are aware and can respond if appropriate.
Threat Management Summary	This widget provides an overview of how your organization was protected over the past seven days. It will show a breakdown of malware, phishing, and Office 365 ATP protections based on your licensing.
Threat Protection Status	This widget shows trends of phishing and malware.
Global Weekly Threat Detections	This widget summarizes scanned messages, the breakdown of the scan (including safe messages), and messages that were blocked.
Malware	This widget shows detected malware trends and families.
Insights	This widget shows key issues you should review, including top targeted users, as well as recommendations and actions you should take.
Threat Investigation & Response	This widget is included with Office 365 ATP Plan 2 and helps to identify emerging campaigns, to investigate threats, and to manage incidents.
Trends	This widget shows a detailed breakdown of messaging in your environment.

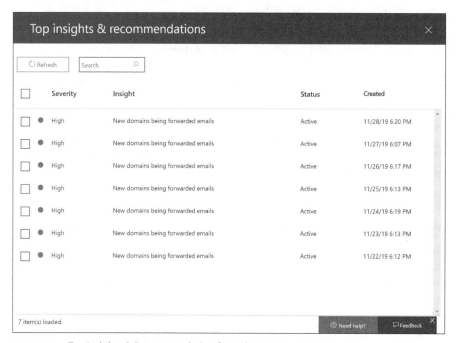

FIGURE 4-1 Top Insights & Recommendation from the Security Dashboard

You can click any report in the dashboard to view more details about the report and to create a schedule to automatically email the report to you on a regular basis (see Figure 4-2). You can also view **Related Reports**, which appear at the lower-left portion of the screen.

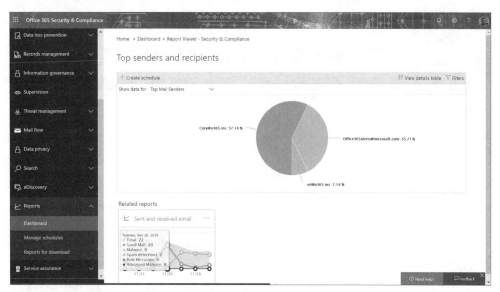

FIGURE 4-2 Top Senders And Recipients from the Office 365 Security & Compliance Dashboard, with the related Sent And Received Email report below

Plan for custom security reporting with Intelligent Security Graph

You can also create your own custom security reports by directly querying the Intelligent Security Graph, as shown in Figure 4-3. This is useful when an included report does not exist or does not have the level of detail you want for some internal reporting needs. The Security API is a REST API that developers can query to build their own solutions; this can be done either for the developers' own internal teams or by using third-party products. Existing third-party solutions can query the API, or you can develop your own using Python, ASP.Net, or other languages. If your security team is developing its own tools or looking at third-party security tools, you should consider whether they can integrate with Office 365 to provide more functionality.

> **NEED MORE REVIEW?** **USING A NEW API**
>
> Consult *https://www.microsoft.com/security/blog/2018/04/17/connect-to-the-intelligent-security-graph-using-a-new-api/* for more information on this.

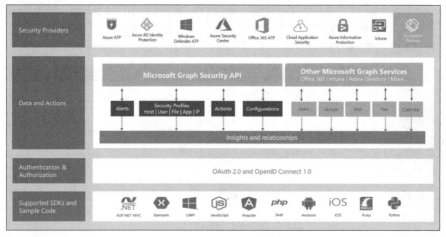

FIGURE 4-3 Architectural overview of the Intelligent Security Graph

Review Office 365 Secure Score actions and recommendations

One of the most important things Microsoft includes with Office 365 is the Microsoft Secure Score. The term "Secure Score" used to be referred to as the "Office 365 Secure Score," and you might still encounter that name on the exam. No matter what you call it, your Secure Score is a measurement of your security posture, and it evaluates what security options you have based on your licensing and how well or thoroughly you have deployed them. The higher your score, the more fully you have deployed all the available security solutions and the more resistant your organization should be to attempts to compromise it through your Microsoft cloud services. Secure Score helps you to:

- Evaluate the current state of your security posture
- Identify ways to improve your security posture
- Compare your posture with benchmarks and KPIs

The idea is to help you to identify actions you can take and settings you can enable to better secure your environment. Secure Score is regularly updated as new capabilities are released and should be checked by administrators at least monthly. You should aspire to a higher score while balancing security with the business needs of your organization. Figure 4-4 shows an example of a Secure Score.

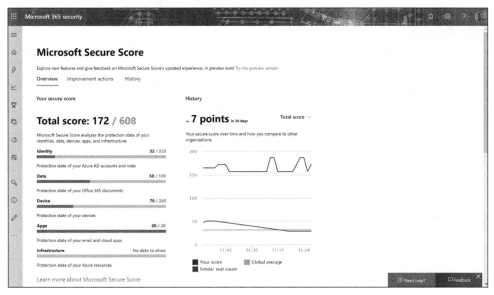

FIGURE 4-4 Microsoft Secure Score

Several roles have access to Secure Score. Roles that have read and write access can make changes to Secure Score, acknowledge recommendations, and note recommendations that are handled through third-party solutions or are accepted risks in the environment. Read-only roles can only view the reports. The following read and write roles are available:

- Global Administrator
- Security Administrator
- Exchange Administrator
- SharePoint Administrator

The following read-only roles are available:

- Helpdesk Admin
- User Account Admin
- Service Support Admin
- Security Reader
- Security Operator
- Global Reader

Microsoft Secure Score is not limited to only Office 365. It includes information from all the Microsoft cloud services your organization uses and includes what is being evaluated, what the current state is, and the actions you can take to improve the security of the services in question. Items evaluated are broken into four groups:

- Identity
- Data

- Device
- Applications

Infrastructure Items are presented in a table with a number of headers and can be sorted based on the significance of the improvement, the relative complexity to implement or deploy, and the potential impact to users. To get some "quick wins," administrators should look at what can be implemented and focus on things that have a higher effect on the Secure Score and a lower effect on users and then move on to those things that might affect users. One of the most important things you can do to improve your Secure Score is to implement multifactor authentication (MFA) for everyone. This is separated into Require MFA For Azure AD Privileged Roles (see Figure 4-5) and Require MFA For All Users because it's relatively easy to get admins to use MFA, but it is somewhat more difficult to do so for users.

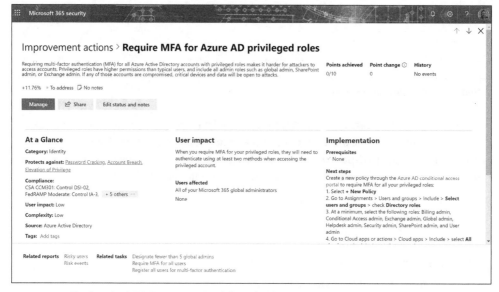

FIGURE 4-5   The Require MFA For Azure AD Privileged Roles Improvement Action

From the recommendations, you can see steps for implementing the recommended settings, post notes about the topic, and in many cases, link directly to the action you need to take to enable the setting. Click the **Edit Status And Notes** button to see a **Choose Status** option from which you can choose one of the following statuses (see Figure 4-6):

- To Address
- Planned
- Risk Accepted
- Resolved Through Third Party

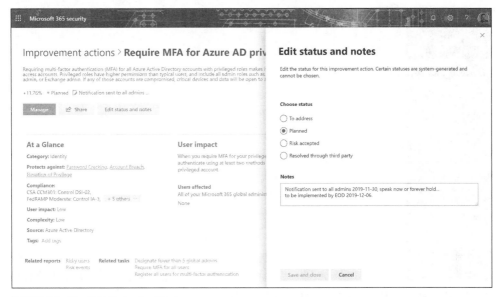

FIGURE 4-6 The Edit Status And Notes page

The **Risk Accepted** option will remove the recommendation from your list, while the **Resolved Through Third Party** option will both remove the recommendation and increase your score by the corresponding number of points.

It's important to note that Secure Score evolves over time and will continue to include more recommendations as new capabilities are added. Administrators should review Secure Score regularly and take actions based on the recommendations to improve their security postures.

Configure alert policies in the Office 365 Security and Compliance Center

Alerts are one of the key components of the Office 365 Security and Compliance Center. Administrators can use alerts to monitor activities within their Office 365 environments and to be notified when events occur or policies are violated so that they can take action or follow-up on actions that were automatically taken, such as when a user attempts to send data in an email and DLP prevents the email from being sent. There are four subsections within Alerts: Dashboard, View Alerts, Alert Policies, and Manage Advanced Alerts.

Dashboard

The dashboard is the top level of Alerts and includes graphical charts of Alert Trends, Active Alerts By Severity, Recent Alerts, Alert Policies, and Other Alerts, as shown in Figure 4-7. Administrators and Security Operators can use this page to get a snapshot of what is happening or has recently happened within the environment.

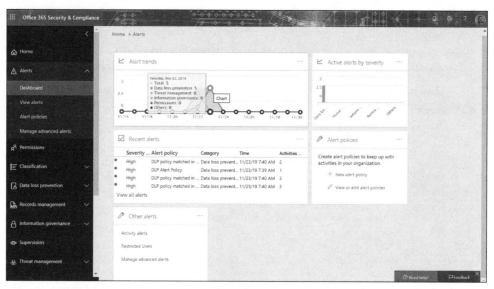

FIGURE 4-7 The Alerts Dashboard showing recent activity

View alerts

The View Alerts section shown in Figure 4-8 provides you with a view of all alerts that have triggered in your Office 365 tenant, including both those triggered by default alert policies and those triggered by alert policies you have created yourself.

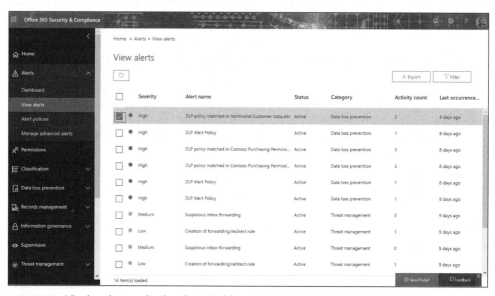

FIGURE 4-8 Viewing alerts under the Alerts Dashboard, showing details for all active alerts

You can filter and export the alerts; sort them based on **Severity**, **Status**, **Last Occurrence**, and **Activity Count**. You can view details and take actions based on internal policies and responses. When you click an alert, you can see more details, update the status, and add comments to the alert; when appropriate, you can resolve the alert. Figure 4-9 shows the expanded view of an alert.

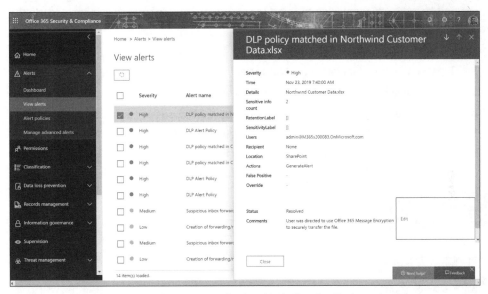

FIGURE 4-9   Editing an alert to indicate it is resolved and including details about the alert

Once resolved, the alert will not display because the default filter is set to not show resolved alerts. Click the filter and select **Resolved** to see the details, including who changed the status and when. After setting the filter to **Resolved**, it will appear as shown in Figure 4-10.

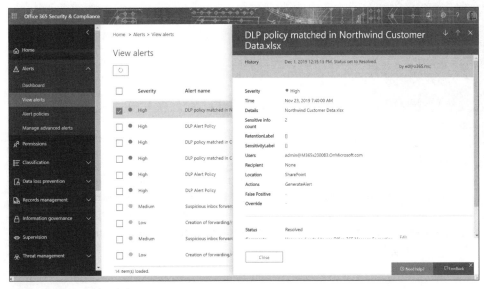

FIGURE 4-10   A resolved alert

Alert policies

Alert policies include several default alerts, as well as alerts you can create yourself. Default alerts are identified as System Alerts, while alerts you create are identified as Custom Alerts. Alerts include categories for filtering and can include actions beyond just appearing in the Alerts dashboard, such as emailing the alert to users or groups. To create a custom alert, do the following:

1. Click the **+New Alert Policy** button.
2. Type a name for your alert in the **Name** field. Try to be descriptive but brief.
3. Use the **Description** box to add more details.
4. From the **Severity** drop-down menu, select **Low**, **Medium**, or **High**. Consider events that can lead to data loss or leakage to be **High**, while informational events are **Low**.
5. In the **Category** drop-down menu shown in Figure 4-11, choose **Data Loss Prevention**, **Threat Management**, **Information Governance**, **Permissions**, **Mail Flow**, or **Others**.

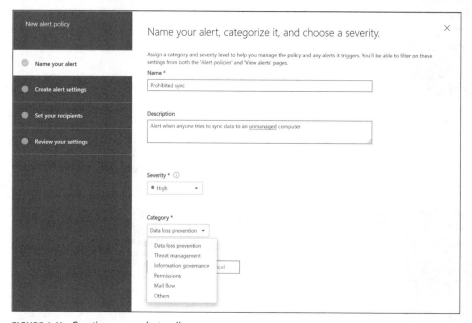

FIGURE 4-11 Creating a new alert policy

6. Click **Next**.
7. Under **Activity Is**, select the type of activity for which you wish to receive an alert, and if necessary, add conditions by clicking the **Add A Condition** drop-down menu. Conditions are context-aware, and can include things like **IP Addresses**, **File Name**, **User**, and the like. Note that these are optional and intended to help you create more specific alerts where desired.

8. Under **How Do You Want The Alert To Be Triggered?**, select the frequency for triggering the alert, as shown in Figure 4-12. Click **Next**.

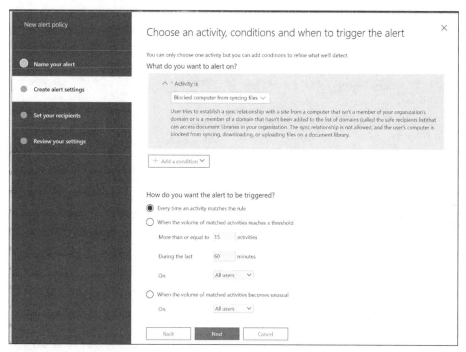

FIGURE 4-12 Choosing the activity

9. Enter the email recipients who should receive email alerts (if desired) and any daily notification limit. Click **Next**.

10. Review your settings, edit any necessary, and then click **Finish**. By default, the rule will be enabled, but you can also choose to leave it disabled.

Manage advanced alerts

If your tenant has licenses for Microsoft Cloud App Security (MCAS) included in Microsoft 365 E5, you can manage advanced alerts that are triggered by detections in MCAS. This section includes a shortcut to launch the Cloud App Security portal. MCAS is covered in Chapter 3, "Implement and manage information protection."

> **REAL WORLD ALERTS AND EMAIL**
>
> Many admins use the alert emails with their help desk ticketing systems to send alerts to email addresses, which automatically creates tickets, rather than sending emails directly to specific users or groups of users. While managing alerts in the console is fine, if you already have an existing system, you can use email alerts to push tickets to your existing systems, or you can use the Graph API to pull alerts.

Skill 4.2: Manage and analyze audit logs and reports

By default, auditing of administrative actions is enabled in Office 365, but there is much more you should audit, and you should also ensure that the audit logs are reviewed regularly. You can use the Search & Compliance Center or PowerShell to configure and search the unified audit log, which retains data for 90 days. If your organization needs to retain audit data for longer than this, you can download the audit logs or import them into Azure Log Analytics for longer retention.

In this skill, we will review how to manage and analyze audit logs and reports.

> **In this skill, you learn how to:**
> - Plan for auditing and reporting
> - Configure Office 365 auditing and reporting
> - Perform audit log search
> - Review and interpret compliance reports and dashboards
> - Configure audit alert policy

Plan for auditing and reporting

Auditing activities by administrators and reviewing those activities regularly is a critical part of ensuring security and compliance. Many organizations audit activities but far fewer actually review those logs, which is why the average time an attacker has access to a network before detection is 90 days or longer. The unified audit log can be used to review or search for both administrator and user activities across your Microsoft Office 365 organization.

Following are the specific categories of action categories that are logged:

- Azure Active Directory
- Exchange Online
- SharePoint Online
- OneDrive for Business
- Sway
- PowerBI
- Microsoft Teams
- Yammer

The following user activities are logged:

- Exchange Online
- SharePoint Online
- OneDrive for Business
- Sway
- PowerBI
- Microsoft Teams
- Yammer

REAL WORLD **MAILBOX AUDITING**

By default, admin auditing is enabled and cannot be disabled, but until recently, user auditing of mailboxes had to be enabled. In 2018, Microsoft began to enable user auditing on mailboxes by default. Administrators can configure or even disable user auditing if they choose to do so.

It's important to note that events are not logged in real-time. For many of the services, there can be up to a 30-minute delay between an event happening and it appearing in the audit log; for Azure Active Directory and other services, the delay can be up to 24 hours. Audit logging is not intended to be used to perform troubleshooting or real-time alerting. It is intended to provide a record of actions that were taken.

By default, Global Administrators and Security Administrators have the permissions necessary to configure auditing and to view audit logs. Also, there are several built-in roles that have the permissions to search the audit logs:

- Compliance Administrator
- Compliance Data Administrator
- Organization Management
- Security Operator

There is also a View-Only Audit Logs role that can be used if you need to assign users only the ability to view audit logs through RBAC. For users who are not explicitly added to the Exchange Organization Management role, you need to assign additional permissions in the Exchange Admin Center so that these users can run the Exchange cmdlets needed to search the audit log. To assign a role to a user, open the Security & Compliance Center and choose **Permissions**. You can select one of the existing roles, or you can create a new one. Browse to **Permissions**, click the **+Create** button, and follow the wizard. From the **Choose Roles** window shown in Figure 4-13, assign them either the **View-Only Audit Logs** or the **Audit Logs** roles.

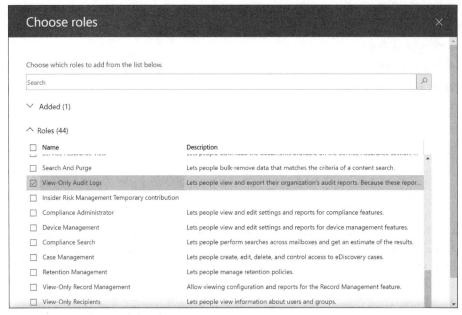

FIGURE 4-13 Assigning the View-Only Audit Logs role

Configure Office 365 auditing and reporting

By default, both administrator audit logging and mailbox auditing are enabled in Office 365, but if your environment was set up before Microsoft made the decision to do this by default, you might need to enable auditing. To fully enable auditing for your Office 365 environment, you can use the Security & Compliance Center:

1. Log in to the Security & Compliance Center at *https://protection.office.com*.

2. Choose **Search & Investigation** > **Audit Log Search**.

3. Select **Start Recording User And Admin Activity**. (Note that if auditing has already been enabled, you will not see this link.)

Then for mailbox auditing, which again is now enabled by default, you can check the status of your users' mailboxes using PowerShell. Connect to Exchange Online using Remote Power-Shell and run this command:

```
Get-OrganizationConfig | fl AuditDisabled
```

If this command returns *False*, then mailbox auditing is enabled in your tenant. If this command returns *True*, you should run the following two commands:

```
Set-OrganizationConfig -AuditDisabled:$False
Get-Mailbox -ResultSize Unlimited -Filter{RecipientTypeDetails -eq "UserMailbox"} | Set-
    Mailbox -AuditEnabled$true.
```

The first command enables auditing for all new mailboxes going forward, and the second command enables auditing on all existing user mailboxes.

Once enabled, you use the Security & Compliance Center to search the audit logs.

Perform audit log search

The audit log search tool is located in the Security & Compliance Center and is used to search for and export information from the audit logs. Global Administrators have rights to search audit logs, as do Compliance Management and Organization Management roles. If you are not in one of these roles, you must be granted either the View-Only Audit Logs or the Audit Logs role in Exchange Online, where these permissions are controlled.

To search the audit logs, follow these steps:

1. Log in to the **Security & Compliance Center** at *https://protection.office.com*.

2. In the left panel, click **Search**, and then choose **Audit Log Search**. By default, the search can show results for all activities for the past seven days. You can expand the Activities drop-down menu to see the full list of activities that you can review. (See Figure 4-14.)

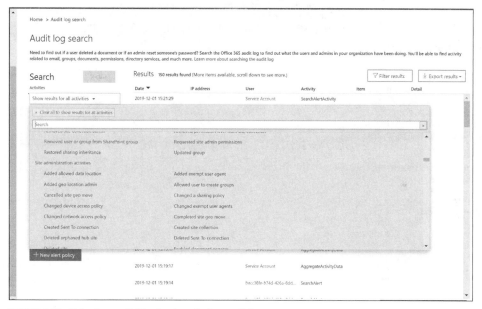

FIGURE 4-14   Selecting activities to show in the audit log

You can also specify date and time ranges, specific users, and key words, such as partial filenames or URLs.

> **REAL WORLD**   **A LOT OF INFORMATION IS AUDITED**
>
> There are scores of events that are audited, and many of those events have several type codes to specify what sort of event occurred. It's beyond both the scope of this book and the exam to detail every option, but you will want to review *https://docs.microsoft.com/en-us/microsoft-365/compliance/detailed-properties-in-the-office-365-audit-log* to become more familiar with everything that is audited. You should also review *https://docs.microsoft.com/en-us/microsoft-365/compliance/enable-mailbox-auditing* for specific details about mailbox auditing.

Review and interpret compliance reports and dashboards

The Compliance Manager portal used to be a part of the Security & Compliance Center, but it is now its own portal at *https://servicetrust.microsoft.com*. This standalone portal provides a simplified experience for managing compliance. You might still see references to the original location in the Security & Compliance Center, but it is no longer accessible. You can read about the new Microsoft Compliance Score (Preview) at *https://docs.microsoft.com/en-us/micro-soft-365/compliance/compliance-score*.

To use the Compliance Manager portal, you must have the appropriate permissions. Built-in roles and their permissions include those shown in Table 4-3.

TABLE 4-3 Built-in admin roles

	Compliance Manager Reader	Compliance Manager Contributor	Compliance Manager Assessor	Compliance Manager Administrator	Portal Admin
Read Data: Users can read but not edit data.	X	X	X	X	X
Edit Data: Users can edit all fields, except the Test Result and Test Date fields.		X	X	X	X
Edit Test Results: Users can edit the Test Result and Test Date fields.			X	X	X
Manage Assessments: Users can create, archive, and delete Assessments.				X	X
Manage Users: Users can add other users in their organizations to the Reader, Contributor, Assessor, and Administrator roles. Only those users with the Global Administrator role in your organization can add or remove users from the Portal Admin role.					X

At the time this book was written, the exam focused on the older Compliance Manager. However, the purpose of the old and new compliance tools is the same: to help customers manage their regulatory compliances such that they are responsible for some aspects, while Microsoft is responsible for others. Assessments are the core component and are used to measure the service against a certification standard or regulation. Assessments consist of the following:

- **In-Scope Services.** This lists in-scope service, as well as the services to which they are specific.

- **Microsoft-Managed Controls.** This lists what Microsoft is responsible for as the data custodian/service provider.

- **Control ID.** This is the specific section or article number of the certification or regulation.

- **Title.** This is from the certification or regulation.

- **Article ID.** This is the GDPR article number if the control is related to GDPR.

- **Description.** This is just a text description.

- **Compliance Score.** This is a value from 1 to 10 and indicates the level of risk associated with non-compliance. The higher the value, the greater the risk. This is also color-coded from yellow, orange, and through red.

- **More.** This expands to provide greater detail including audit results.

Figure 4-15 shows the original Compliance Manager dashboard.

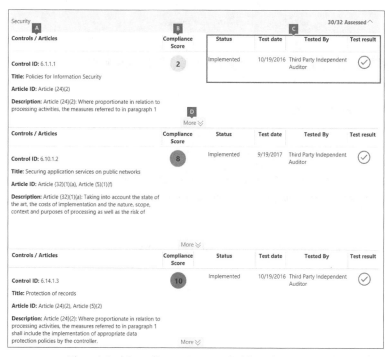

FIGURE 4-15   The original Compliance Manager dashboard

The Compliance Score, as shown in Figure 4-16, provides a visual indicator of how your organization is doing on compliance with relevant standards based on what Microsoft has completed and what your organization has indicated as being complete in the Compliance Manager.

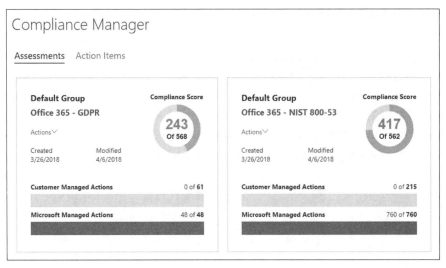

FIGURE 4-16 Compliance Score in the Compliance Manager

MORE INFO

You can read more about the Microsoft Compliance Manager (Classic) at *https://docs. microsoft.com/en-us/microsoft-365/compliance/meet-data-protection-and-regulatory-reqs- using-microsoft-cloud.*

Compliance Manager includes preconfigured templates for the following:

- ISO 27001: 2013
- ISO 27018: 2014
- NIST 800-53 Rev. 4
- NIST 800-171
- NIST Cybersecurity Framework (CSF)
- Cloud Security Alliance (CSA) Cloud Controls Matrix (CCM) 3.0.1
- Federal Financial Institutions Examination Council (FFIEC) Information Security Booklet
- HIPAA / HITECH
- FedRAMP Moderate
- European Union GDPR
- California Consumer Privacy Act (CCPA) Preview
- Microsoft 365 Data Protection Baseline

Configure audit alert policy

Audit alert policies can be configured to generate alerts when certain audit events take place. You can create these alerts so that you are notified, rather than having to review the audit logs. Details are still logged and can be searched after the fact. To configure audit alert policies, do the following:

1. Log in to the Security & Compliance Center at *https://protection.office.com*.
2. Click **Search** > **Audit Log Search**.
3. At the bottom of that page, click the **+New Alert Policy** button (see Figure 4-17).

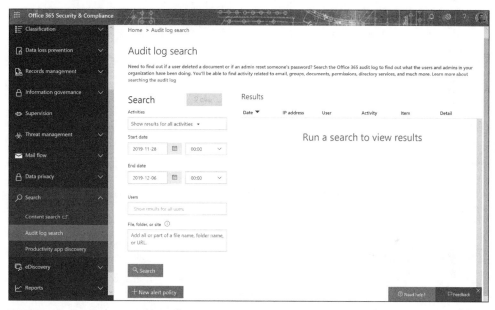

FIGURE 4-17   Creating a new alert policy

4. Give the alert a name in the **Name** field and enter something into the **Description** field to help you understand what it is, why it is there, and who created it.
5. Set the **Alert Type** to **Custom** and select the **Activities** for which you wish to generate an alert.
6. The default setting, **Show Results For All Users**, is usually appropriate. You can set specific users if that is really valid for an audit alert.
7. In the **Recipients** field, enter the email address(es) to which to send the alert, as shown in Figure 4-18.
8. Click **Save**.

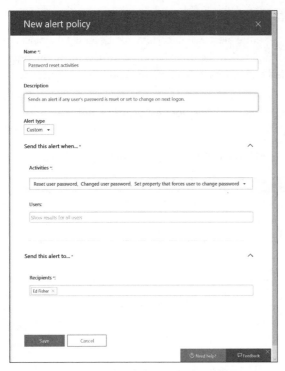

FIGURE 4-18 Entering details for a new alert policy

Skill 4.3: Configure Office 365 classification and labeling

Classification and labeling are used to classify and protect sensitive content while still supporting your users' ability to be productive and to collaborate with others. Sensitivity Labels in Office 365 can do the following:

- Enforce protection settings, including encryption and watermarks
- Protect content in Office applications
- Enforce restrictions on data accessed by mobile devices using endpoint protection in Microsoft Intune
- Protect content when using third-party services using Cloud App Security
- Classify data for usage reporting

In this skill, you learn how to:

- Plan for data governance classification and labels
- Search for personal data
- Apply labels to personal data
- Monitor for leaks of personal data
- Create and publish Office 365 labels
- Configure label policies

Plan for data governance classification and labels

Organizations create, store, manage, and dispose of many different types of data that falls under many different sets of requirements, including business processes, laws and regulations, and compliance standards. Sometimes, the same data might fall under differing requirements. Documents related to employment contracts or to support compliance might need to be maintained as immutable records, while business plans for mergers and acquisitions or patent applications might need to be protected much more strenuously than marketing materials.

Many organizations either struggle with manually dealing with classifications and labels, or they do nothing about it at all, relying upon users to keep the right data in the right place and to exercise caution when storing and sharing the data. The risk there is that a user might make the wrong decision or fail to make any decision at all, jeopardizing the data in question. Data governance uses labels that can be manually or automatically applied to data, so proper permissions, restrictions, and encryption can be handled with a minimum of effort. Manual labeling relies upon users making the determination of what needs to be done with data, while automatic labeling can be applied when data contains certain conditions that can be matched, such as key words or tags in the metadata. Also, organizations might need to identify and classify certain data as records, which indicates the data not only must be retained but that it cannot be modified.

Administrators need to work with various people in their organization to develop the requirements' classifications based on departmental, regulatory, or legal requirements. Some of the departments that will be involved can include human resources and legal, both of which will likely create large amounts of data that must be classified correctly. Larger organizations might have a data protection officer or department responsible for defining the requirements and ensuring they are met.

Without a good user training program that is regularly reinforced, relying upon users to apply manual labels might not be the best course of action, so it can be well worth the additional licensing costs to use automatic labeling available in Office 365 E5, Microsoft 365 E5, and the Advanced Compliance add-on license.

Search for personal data

"Personal data" does not refer to data such as a user's personal photos or MP3 collection; instead, it refers to data that falls under the scope of Article 4 of the General Data Privacy Regulation

(GDPR) as any data that relates to a resident of the European Union (EU). It can be data that identifies a person or data that can be used to identify a person. Sensitive information types in Office 365 are used to define personal data, including things like national ID numbers and health care numbers.

You can use Content Search to find personal data stored within SharePoint Online and OneDrive for Business, and you can leverage sensitive information types with DLP to find personal data in transit sent through Exchange Online. You can also search on keywords, dates, and other metadata. There are several specific sensitive information types for EU citizen data, including:

- Belgium National Number
- Credit Card Number
- Croatia Identity Card Number
- Croatia Personal Identification (OIB) Number
- Czech National Identity Card Number
- Denmark Personal Identification Number
- EU Debit Card Number
- Finland National ID
- Finland Passport Number
- France Driver's License Number
- France National ID Card (CNI)
- France Passport Number
- France Social Security Number (INSEE)
- German Driver's License Number
- Germany Identity Card Number
- German Passport Number
- Greece National ID Card
- International Banking Account Number (IBAN)
- IP Address
- Ireland Personal Public Service (PPS) Number
- Italy's Driver's License Number
- Netherlands Citizen's Service (BSN) Number
- Norway Identity Number
- Poland Identity Card
- Poland National ID (PESEL)
- Poland Passport
- Portugal Citizen Card Number
- Spain Social Security Number (SSN)
- Sweden National ID
- Sweden Passport Number

- U.K. Driver's License Number
- U.K. Electoral Roll Number
- U.K. National Health Service Number
- U.K. National Insurance Number (NINO)
- U.S./U.K. Passport Number

More will be added soon. You can enhance the search types using count ranges, and confidence ranges if you need to specify a certain number of results or if you wish to tune your search in the event you get either too few or too many results.

To search for personal data within Office 365, follow these steps:

1. Log in to the Security & Compliance Center at *https://protection.office.com*.
2. Expand **Search** and then click **Content Search**.
3. Click the **+New Search** button.
4. In the **Search Query** dialog box, the default search is for *Keywords*. In the **Keywords** section of the dialog box shown in Figure 4-19, enter the content search query for the sensitive information type you wish to find. For example, to find documents that include at least 5 credit card numbers with an 85 percent or better certainty, use this query:
   `SensitiveType:"Credit Card Number|5|85.."`

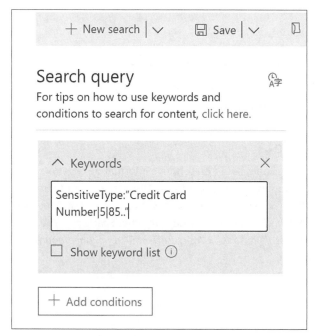

FIGURE 4-19 Entering details for a new search query

5. Make sure the **Specific Locations** option is selected and click **Modify** (see Figure 4-20).
6. Scroll down and enable **SharePoint Sites**.

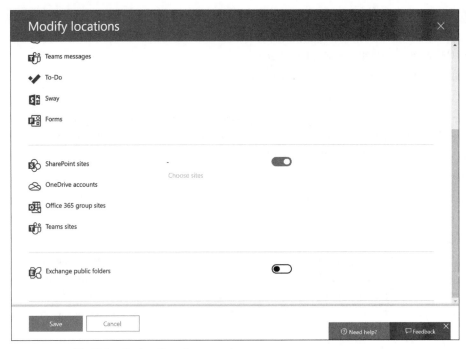

FIGURE 4-20 Modifying the locations for a search

7. Click **Save** > **Save & Run**.

8. Give your search a **Name** and a **Description** and then click **Save**.

9. The search will begin immediately and return results once it is complete.

10. You can view the results or export them if desired.

Apply labels to personal data

Retention labels can be applied to personal data based on sensitive information types or other factors, such as names or locations. You can use labels to perform eDiscovery and Content Searches and apply Data Loss Prevention (DLP) policies to protect sensitive data. Use Sensitivity Labels with data stored on-premises with Exchange Online and with other SaaS apps. You can read more about this at *https://docs.microsoft.com/en-us/microsoft-365/compliance/apply-labels-to-personal-data-in-office-365*.

Monitor for leaks of personal data

There are three ways you can monitor for leaks of personal data:

- Office 365 Data Loss Prevention (DLP)
- Office 365 audit log alert policies
- Microsoft Cloud App Security

Create and publish Office 365 labels

You can create and publish both Sensitivity and Retention labels in your environment to make them available to users for manual labeling of files. You create labels and define the settings they apply and restrictions they enforce. You then publish the labels in a policy so that they can be manually applied by users or automatically applied.

To create a Sensitivity Label, do the following:

1. Log in to the Security & Compliance Center at *https://protection.office.com*.

2. In the left panel, expand **Classification** and then click **Sensitivity Labels** (see Figure 4-21).

3. Click the **+Create A Label** button.

4. Give the label a short, intuitive name, and enter text in the **Tooltip** box that will help users understand what the label is for. You can also add a **Description** for admins and then click **Next**.

5. If required, enable **Encryption**. You can choose to assign permissions now or let users assign permissions when they apply the label. If you choose to assign permissions now, you have the option to expire the content and to decide whether to permit offline access. Then you assign permissions as appropriate and click **Next**.

6. You can enable **Content Marking** and add a watermark, header, and/or footer. Customize to meet your needs and then click **Next**.

7. Enable **Endpoint Data Loss Prevention**, if required, and then click **Next**.

8. If you wish to auto-label content, enable it here. Note that you must have either Office 365 ProPlus or the Azure Information Protection Unified Labeling content installed. Also, encryption can both incur a performance hit and limit some other functionality, such as searches. If you are going to auto-label, add the Condition, Accuracy, and Instance Counts desired.

9. Configure whether to auto apply the label or to recommend that users manually apply the label. Enter **Policy Tip** text that will help the user understand the requirement and then click **Next**.

10. If necessary, review the **Auto-Labeling For Office Apps** setting and click **Submit**.

11. Click **Done**.

FIGURE 4-21 A Sensitivity Label

You will see the label in the list. To use it, select the label and click **Publish Labels**; this will launch the wizard to create a label policy, which is covered in the next section.

Configure label policies

Publishing Sensitivity Labels enables them to be used; before publishing, they are not available to users. To publish a label, do the following:

1. Log in to the Security & Compliance Center at *https://protection.office.com*.

2. Browse to **Center** > **Classification** > **Sensitivity Labels** and select the label you want to publish.

3. Click the **Publish Labels** button. At this point, you can only publish one label at a time.

4. On the next screen, you have the option to edit the label if necessary. To publish it, click the **Publish Label** button.

5. On the **Chooses Labels To Publish** screen, you can click **Edit** to add additional labels to publish if necessary. Click **Next**.

6. Choose the users and groups to whom you want to publish the label. By default, **All** is selected, but you can publish only to specific users or groups if a label is only suitable for some users. When you're ready, click **Next**.

7. Set the options for **Policy Settings** that are appropriate for your label, including whether it should be applied by default; if users must provide a justification before removing or selecting a lower classification; or whether users must apply some label. You can also add a link to a custom help page, such as an internal SharePoint Online page. When you are ready, click **Next**.

8. Give the policy a **Name** and a **Description**. It's suggested that you name the policy for the label and add a description that is informative for users. Click **Next**.

9. As shown in Figure 4-22, review your settings, edit any if necessary, click **Submit**, and then click **Done**.

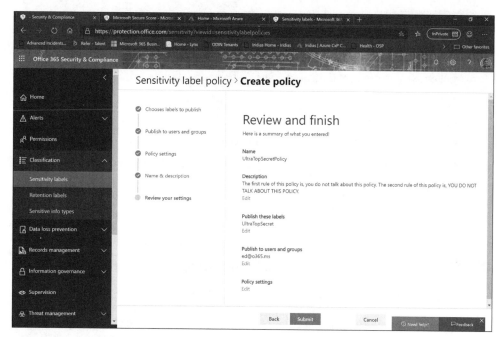

FIGURE 4-22 Sensitivity Label Policy

It can take up to an hour before the policy is available to users.

Skill 4.4: Manage data governance and retention

Data governance and retention focus on ensuring that organizations keep what they need and can get rid of what they no longer need; more importantly, they allow organizations to rid themselves of what they don't want to keep around anymore. Many laws, regulations, and compliance standards set requirements for how long certain types of data must be kept, while the litigious nature of business leads some companies to minimize how much data is just lying around and for how long it remains lying around. That's where data governance and retention come into play. Data governance helps you keep what you want and get rid of what you don't. Retention policies help to ensure that data is maintained for the required period of time and can make that data immutable when necessary. Once the retention period is over, retention policies can either relax and allow users to keep or delete data as they wish, or businesses can then delete the data, so it is no longer available.

Plan for data governance and retention

Organizations create, store, manage, and dispose of many different types of data that falls under many different sets of requirements, including business processes, laws and regulations, and compliance standards. Sometimes, the same data might fall under differing requirements. For example, in the United States, payroll records must be maintained for three years according to federal regulations, while in California they must be maintained for six years. Payroll tax records need to be maintained for four years. Some organizations might also determine that they need to ensure certain data is not maintained after a period of time. It might be that the data is no longer relevant and those companies don't want to allocate space to store and back it up, or it might be that maintaining certain data beyond a specific period of time could expose them to legal risk from discovery if litigation occurs.

Many organizations either struggle with manually dealing with this, or they do nothing about it, allowing data to accumulate and consume ever-increasing amounts of storage space. Data governance uses labels that can be manually or automatically applied to data so that proper storage and proper disposal can be handled with a minimum of effort. Using labels, data can be identified such that both the retention and the disposal of data can be enforced. Manual labeling relies upon users making the determination of what needs to be done with data, while automatic labeling can be applied when data contains certain conditions that can be matched, such as keywords or tags in the metadata. Organizations might also need to identify and classify certain data as records, which indicates the data must be retained and that it cannot be modified.

Administrators need to work with others in their organizations to develop the requirements for retention and disposal based on departmental, regulatory, or legal requirements. Both human resources and legal departments will likely create large amounts of data that must be retained and disposed of in a timely fashion. Larger organizations might have data retention officers or departments responsible for defining the requirements and ensuring they are met.

Data can only be tagged with one retention label. Manual labels take precedence over automatic labels, and the longest retention period takes precedence over shorter retention periods, so it's important to plan out labels that are well-named and meet the requirements for your data governance program. Without a good user training program that is regularly re-inforced, relying upon users to apply manual labels might not be the best course of action. This means it can be well worth the additional licensing costs to use automatic labeling available in Office 365 E5, Microsoft 365 E5, and the Advanced Compliance add-on license.

Review and interpret data governance reports and dashboards

The Security & Compliance Center includes an Information Governance section, and within this section, administrators can find the Information Governance dashboard and the Label Activity Explorer. The first thing to notice is the Information Governance toolbox, which is a wizard-driven interface for importing data into Office 365. Here, you can create and publish labels, configure retention and supervision policies, and set up monitoring and alerts. Because this is a very useful tool for administrators who are starting out with Office 365, we will cover each of these functions separately.

The Information Governance dashboard shown in Figure 4-23 includes several graphical reports, which will help you understand how to classify your data, identify data that is being retained, and see users who are retaining data. It also highlights the top labels used in your environment, recommendations for content that might need to be retained, and your trending data consumption.

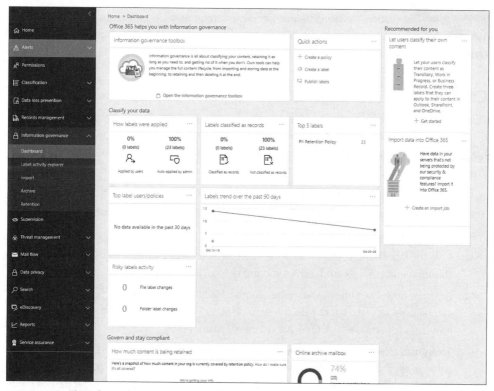

FIGURE 4-23 The Information Governance dashboard

Each of the sections can be clicked to drill deeper into the data, view reports, and filter if required. Figure 4-24 shows **Label Usage Over The Past 90 Days**. Related reports help administrators see what is happening in their environments.

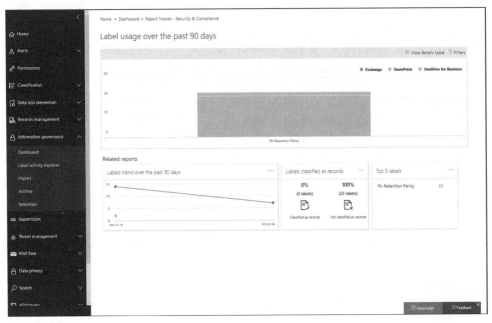

FIGURE 4-24   A report on Label Usage Over The Past 90 Days

Configure retention policies

The process of creating a retention label is very similar to creating Sensitivity Labels. You can do this under the **Information Governance** section of the Security & Compliance Center, or the **Classification** section. We'll use the **Classification** section because it has a more intuitive layout. The process when doing this in the Information governance section is similar:

1. Log in to the Security & Compliance Center at *https://protection.office.com*.

2. In the left panel, expand **Classification** and then click **Retention Labels**.

3. Click the **+Create A Label** button.

4. Give the label a short, intuitive name. You can also add descriptions for admins and users, though neither is required. When you are ready, click **Next**.

5. If you want the retention label to be automatically applied, enter one or more values that can be used to match data with the requirement. You can use existing values or create new ones for your tenant. Click **Next** when you are ready.

6. To enforce retention, click the **Retention** button to turn on retention, and configure the settings as required. Note that once a retention period passes, you can choose to delete the data, trigger a disposition review, or do nothing. You can also choose to allow data to be deleted at any time or to automatically delete the data when it reaches a certain age based on

its original creation time, its last modification time, the time it was labeled, or upon an event occurring. If you need to designate data as a record, which means it must be retained and cannot be modified, check the **Use Label To Classify Content As A Record**. Click **Next**.

7. Review your settings, as shown in Figure 4-25, and then click **Create This Label**.

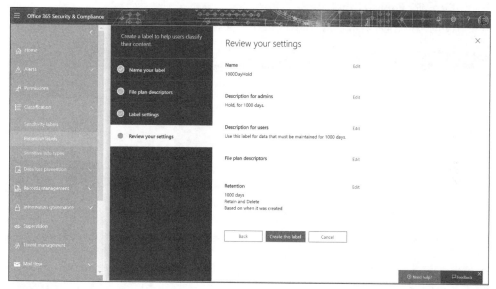

FIGURE 4-25 Creating a retention label

As with Sensitivity Labels, you need to publish a retention label before it can be used. You can use the Information Governance portal of the Security & Compliance Center or the Classification section. For this example, we'll use the Classification section because it has a more intuitive layout, though the process for doing this in the Information Governance portal is similar.

Publishing retention labels follows a similar process to publishing Sensitivity Labels:

1. Log in to the Security & Compliance Center at *https://protection.office.com*.

2. Expand **Classification** and click **Retention Labels**.

3. Select the label you want to publish. A new screen will appear for the retention label with the name of the retention label you selected.

4. Review the settings and edit if necessary. When you are ready, click the **Publish Label** button.

5. On the **Choose Labels To Publish** screen, you can click **Edit** to add additional labels to publish if necessary. Click **Next**.

6. Choose the locations to which you will publish the labels. By default, the option is set to **All Locations**, which includes Content In Exchange Email, Office 365 Groups, and One-Drive and SharePoint Documents. If you only want to apply this retention label in certain locations, you can select **Let Me Choose Specific Locations**. From there, you can select locations or **Users And Groups** to which or whom you want to publish the label. When you're ready, click **Next**.

7. Give the policy a name and a description. It's suggested that you name the policy with a name that includes the label name and that you provide a description that is informative for users. Click **Next**.

8. On the **Review Your Settings** screen, review your settings, edit any if necessary, and then click **Publish Label**.

9. When you select a label, you can see the options to interact with the label in Figure 4-26.

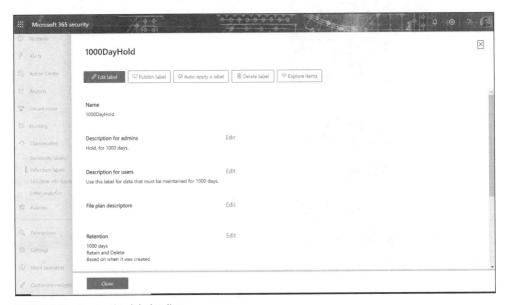

FIGURE 4-26 A retention label policy

Remember, it might take up to an hour before the policy is available to users.

Define data governance event types

In addition to retention based on when something was created or when it was modified, you can take action based on an event. This can be useful in situations such as retaining all data for an employee who leaves the company; in this case, you might want to retain all the employee's data for a specific period of time after the employee leaves, rather than when the data was last modified or created. You might also associate data retention with the expiration of a contract or the end-of-life for a product. You can use existing event types or create your own.

To use event-based retention, you create a label to associate it with an event rather than a time stamp for its creation or its last modification. Finally, you publish a retention label policy in the same way as before. To create an event-based label, do the following:

1. Log in to the Security & Compliance Center at *https://protection.office.com*.

2. In the left panel, expand the **Classification** section and then click **Retention Labels**.

3. Click the **+Create A Label** button.

4. Give the label a short, intuitive name. You can also add descriptions for admins and users, though neither is required. When you are ready, click Next.

5. If you want the retention label to be automatically applied, enter one or more values that can be used to match data with the requirement. You can use existing values or create new ones for your tenant. When you are ready, click **Next**.

6. To enforce retention, click the **Enable Retention** button and configure the settings as required. Note that once a retention period passes, you can choose to delete the data, trigger a disposition review, or do nothing. To see the next two options, either choose to trigger a disposition review or delete the content automatically.

7. From the **Retain Or Delete The Content Based On** drop-down menu, select **An Event**. Then, click **Choose An Event** Type.

8. You can select one of the existing Event types, or you can create a new event type. Choose the desired type, check the box next to it, click **Add**, and then click **Next**.

9. Review your settings, then click **Create This Label**, as shown in Figure 4-27.

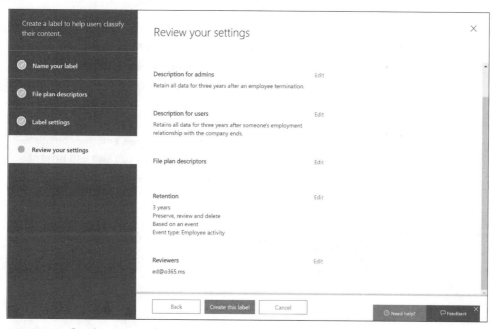

FIGURE 4-27   Creating an event-based retention label

Define data governance supervision policies

Data governance supervision occurs when a manager or an auditor needs to review some or all employee communications. This can be to ensure compliance, for training purposes, as part of an investigation, or other reasons. Supervision is part of Advanced Compliance, and it requires that all users who will be under supervision have a Microsoft 365 E5 license, an Office 365 E5 license, or an Office 365 E3 license with the Advanced Compliance add-on.

To use supervision, you should follow these steps:

1. Create a group for users who will be supervising communications. You can use an existing Office 365 or AD group that is synchronized to Office 365, but you cannot use dynamic groups.

2. To set up and to use supervision, all users must be in the Supervisory Review role group. Log in to the Security & Compliance Center at *https://protection.office.com*, open the **Permissions** pane, and add users to the **Supervisory Review** group.

3. If required, you can create sensitive information types using labels or custom keyword dictionaries to search for specific content, such as customer numbers, product names, or other words/phrases specific to your business. To create a custom dictionary, use a text editor to create a list of terms. Use a new line for each followed by a hard return and save the text file in Unicode/UTF-16 (Little Endian) format.

4. In the Security & Compliance Center, on the left panel, click **Supervision**.

5. Click the **+Create** button to create a new supervisory policy.

6. Give the policy a name and (optionally) a description, and then click **Next**.

7. Add the Supervised users or groups. If you choose a group and want to exempt one or more group members from supervision, you can add those users to the **Non Supervised Users** section. By default, Supervision will apply to email and chat within Office 365, but you can deselect **Chat** if desired. **Email** cannot be deselected. When finished, click **Next**.

8. On the **What Communications Do You Want To Review?** page, external communications (**Inbound** and **Outbound**) are selected by default. You can also add **Internal** communications and deselect **Inbound** and/or **Outbound** if desired. You can also set up conditions by clicking **Add A Condition** if you need to scope your supervision policy (see Figure 4-28).

FIGURE 4-28 Conditions for supervisory policies

9. You can also select the checkboxes next to **Use Match Data Model Condition** and/ or **Use Advanced Sensitive Information Condition**, if required. At the time of this writing, the **Data Model Condition** is set to **Offensive Language**, and the **Advanced Sensitive Information Conditions** include 42 types, as shown in Figure 4-29.

10. Select the options you require and then click **Next**.

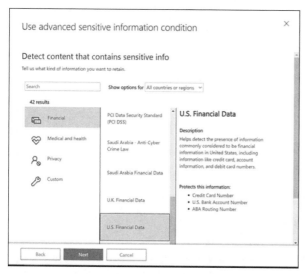

FIGURE 4-29   Use advanced sensitive information condition

11. If you selected **Advanced Sensitive Information**, you can select sensitive information types including **Financial**, **Medical And Health**, **Privacy**, and **Custom Types**. Select what you require and then click **Next**.

12. Enter the percentage of communications you want to review and then click **Next**.

13. Enter the reviewers you want to perform the review, remembering that they need to be in the Supervisory Review group. You need to select the users here because you might have different supervision requirements involving different supervisors. When you are ready, click **Next**.

14. Review your settings, edit if required, and then click **Finish** (see Figure 4-30).

Once you have created a supervisory policy, email should be available for review in the console almost immediately. It can take up to 24 hours for Microsoft Teams instant messages to begin to appear for review. To review, do the following:

1. Log in to the Security & Compliance Center at *https://protection.office.com*.

2. In the left panel, click **Supervision**.

3. Select the **Supervision** policy from the list and then click **Open**.

4. If any communications have taken place that are in scope for the supervision policy, you will see them listed.

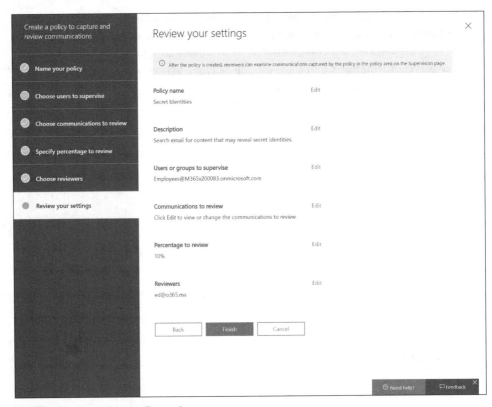

FIGURE 4-30 Supervisory policy settings

Configure information holds

Information holds can be set up using eDiscovery and might be necessary to comply with a regulation or contractual obligation, when investigating an alleged violation of policy, or in response to a court order. You might also choose to put information on hold proactively for certain key employees. Holds are different from retention in that they apply automatically to all data within scope regardless of any tag and might or might not be apparent to the users involved. Users can modify or delete data that is on hold, and that data will appear to be deleted or modified as expected. Versions and deleted items are kept within the system and accessible by administrators using eDiscovery. Each hold is managed as a "case." To configure an information hold, do the following:

1. Log in to the Security & Compliance Center at *https://protection.office.com*.

2. In the left panel, click **eDiscovery** and then click **eDiscovery** again; finally, click the **+Create A Case** button.

3. Enter a case **Name** and **Description** and then click **Save**.

4. From the list of cases, click **Open** next to the case you just created. This will open a new browser tab.

5. Click **Holds**, and then click the **+Create** button.

6. Name your hold, provide a **Description**, and then click **Next**.

7. In the **Choose Locations** dialog box, select the locations where you want to apply the information hold. This can include email, chats, to-do items, data stored in SharePoint Online and OneDrive for Business, Office 365 groups, Teams sites, or in Exchange public folders. When you have made your selection(s), click **Next**.

8. On the **Query Conditions** tab, you can add **Keywords** or use a query to limit the scope of data to be held; or you can leave the **Keywords** and **Conditions** fields blank to hold all data. When you have your options (if any) set, click **Next**.

9. Review your settings, edit if necessary, and then click **Create This Hold**.

Note that, unlike retention, holds have no defined end date. Data is held until you remove or delete the hold.

Import data in the Security and Compliance Center

Administrators can use the Security & Compliance Center to import data, including archived email in legacy PST files and data from social media and instant messaging platforms using connectors. Customers who have existing PST files or third-party archive systems that can export data to PST can import PSTs into archive mailboxes, either over the wire or by shipping hard drives to Microsoft.

Before beginning a PST import, you must be a member of the Import Export role in Exchange Online. Once an account has been added to that role, it can take up to 24 hours before you can create an import job. To import PST data to Office 365, do the following:

1. Log in to the Security & Compliance Center at *https://protection.office.com*.

2. In the left panel, expand **Information Governance** and then click **Import**.

3. Click **Import PST Files**.

4. Click the **+New Import Job** button.

5. Give the job a name and then click **Next**. The name must be all lowercase and may include only letters and numbers. The only other character you can use is a hyphen. Create a name that clearly indicates the purpose of the specific PST import.

6. Select whether you want to import the PSTs over the network or want to ship drives to Microsoft. See the Real World sidebar, "Network versus drive shipping," for the differences. In this example, we will import a PST over the network.

7. Click **Next**.

8. Click **Show Network Upload SAS URL** and copy the URL you will use to upload your data.

9. Click **Download The Azure AzCopy** to download the tool used to copy your PST files.

10. The Azure AzCopy tool will walk you through creating the mapping file you need to map PSTs to individual archive mailboxes and upload the data. When you are done, check both boxes to confirm **I'm Done Uploading My Files** and **I Have Access To The Mapping File**, as shown in Figure 4-31, and then click **Next**.

11. Click the **+Select Mapping File** button to browse to and select the mapping file you used with Azure AzCopy to upload your PST files, and then click **Validate**. When validation is successful, click **Save**.

FIGURE 4-31 Importing PST data to Office 365

REAL WORLD **NETWORK VERSUS DRIVE SHIPPING**

Uploading data has no additional costs but does consume bandwidth. Drive shipping costs money for the service, the hard drives, and the shipping. You will get the drives back once the data is imported, but that's probably not the largest cost. A 1 TB SSD drive costs around US $100, and shipping might cost another US $20, but the import at $2 per GB would be US $2,000! See *https://docs.microsoft.com/en-us/microsoft-365/compliance/use-drive-shipping-to-import-pst-files-to-office-365* for specifics and to weigh the costs of drive shipping against the time it takes to import over the network. It might be slower, but you are dealing with archive data, so it might be worth the wait.

Administrators can also import and archive data on an ongoing basis from the following services:

- **Social media.** Facebook, LinkedIn, Twitter, and Yammer
- **Instant messaging.** Yahoo Messenger, GoogleTalk, and Cisco Jabber
- **Document collaboration.** Box and DropBox
- **Vertical industries.** Customer Relationship Management (such as Salesforce Chatter) and Financial Services (such as Bloomberg and Thomson Reuters)
- **SMS/text messaging.** BlackBerry

Once imported, you can place data on hold and set up auditing and retention policies to maintain this data, even though it originates outside of Office 365. To import data from a web service, you need to set up a connector and a paid Azure subscription. To import data, do the following:

1. Log in to the **Security & Compliance Center** at *https://protection.office.com*.

2. In the left panel, expand **Information Governance** and then click **Import**.

3. Click **Archive Third-Party Data**.

4. Click the **+ Add A Connector** button and choose the service desired. For this example, we will use Twitter.

5. Read and accept the **Terms Of Service**.

6. In the **Add Connector App** window, click the link under **Documentation** to download the step-by-step instructions for the connector.

7. Follow the steps for the specific connector to complete the process.

Configure data archiving

The Security & Compliance Center can be used to enable or disable archive mailboxes for users with at least an Exchange Online Plan 2 license. Once enabled, the default policy moves all content older than one year from the user's primary mailbox to the archive mailbox. You can use retention tags created through the Exchange Admin Center (EAC) to create or modify the default archive policy. To do this, follow these steps:

1. Log in to the EAC at *https://outlook.office.com/ecp*.

2. In the right-hand pane under **Compliance Management**, click **Retention Tags**.

3. Click the **+** sign to create a new tag and select where you want the tag to apply.

4. Give the tag a name, select the **Move To Archive** option, and enter the age in days for when an item should be moved.

5. Enter a comment if desired and then click **Save**.

6. Click Retention Policies.

7. Click the **+** button to add a new retention policy.

8. Give the policy a name, click the **+** sign under **Retention Tags**, and add the retention tag you created.

9. Click **Save** (see Figure 4-32).

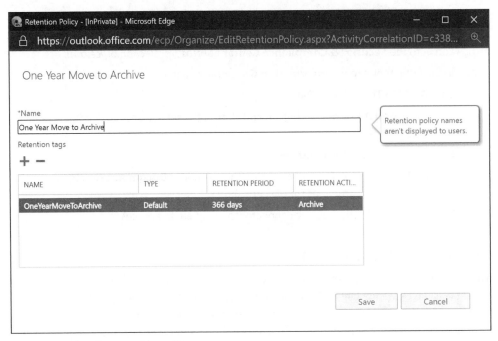

FIGURE 4-32 Creating an archive policy

Manage inactive mailboxes

It's common for organizations to want to maintain ex-employees' mailboxes for ex-employees for a period of time after they leave the company. This might be for compliance, it might be an internal policy, or it might because the employee might return or someone else in the company needs something from the employees' email. Of course, because the user is no longer employed by the organization, it doesn't make sense for that mailbox to remain active, accepting new mail and consuming a license. When you remove a license from a user, delete the user, or (if it is an on-premises object) move the user out of sync scope, the license assigned to that user is returned to the pool of available licenses, and the mailbox is disconnected. The data remains for 30 days, during which time you can restore the user account or map the mailbox to a different account. However, after the 30-day period, if you have done nothing else, the mailbox is gone, and the data is unrecoverable.

If you need to retain the mailbox past the 30-day period, you need to turn the mailbox into an inactive mailbox before you free up the license from the user account. You can place the user on hold or apply a retention policy to the user. An inactive mailbox will be maintained for the duration of the hold or the retention policy and will not consume a license.

There are several things to consider with an inactive mailbox, including the following:

- The user account associated with the mailbox needs to be covered by an Exchange Plan 2 license, which is included in Microsoft 365 E3 and E5 and Office 365 E3 and E5.

- The mailbox cannot be used to send or to receive new email while it is inactive.

- The mailbox is available to be reconnected to a restored user account or a newly created account but is not accessible to any user until it is. Reconnecting to a restored user or connecting it to a new user will again consume a license.

- The mailbox is accessible to eDiscovery searches for the duration of the inactivity period.

- Retention policies can be used to hold only a subset of data, if desired. However, there is a limit of 1,000 maximum mailboxes per policy, so you might need to create multiple policies.

- Some organizations might want to reuse the UPN and/or the SMTP address associated with a former employee. This can have implications for inactive mailboxes. See *https://docs.microsoft.com/en-us/microsoft-365/compliance/inactive-mailboxes-in-office-365* for more on that.

- MRM policies used to delete items will continue to apply. Deleted items will be held in the Recoverable Items folder for the duration of the hold or retention period.

- MRM policies used to move items to the archive are ignored.

EXAM TIP **LITIGATION HOLDS AND RETENTION VERSUS EDISCOVERY CASES AND LABELS**

In theory, you could also use eDiscovery cases or labels to retain data in a mailbox, and if the user account is later deleted, then the mailbox will become an inactive mailbox for the duration of the retention period specified by the label. Microsoft does not recommend using either eDiscovery cases or retention labels to convert a mailbox to an inactive mailbox.

There are four typical management activities involving inactive mailboxes. These include creation and management, changing the hold duration, recovery, and restoration.

Create and manage inactive mailboxes in Office 365

To convert a mailbox to inactive, first confirm the user associated with the mailbox has an appropriate license. Then you can either place the mailbox on litigation hold or apply a retention policy to the mailbox. Both can be set for a limited or unlimited duration. If you are going to use a retention policy, it's best to have a retention policy specifically created and named for the purpose, so you can distinguish it from others. As we previously went over retention policies, here, we will review the steps to place a mailbox on litigation hold:

1. Log in to the Exchange Admin Center at *https://outlook.office.com/ecp*.

2. In the left panel, click **Recipients**, and then at the top, click **Mailboxes**.

3. Find and double-click the mailbox on which you want to put a hold.

4. Click **Mailbox Features**.

5. Scroll down to the **Litigation Hold: Disabled** setting and click **Enable** (see Figure 4-33).

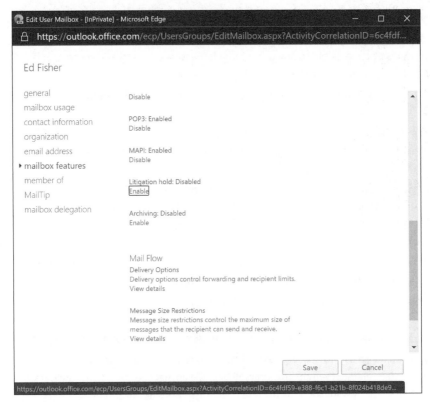

FIGURE 4-33 Enabling litigation hold

6. In the **Litigation Hold Duration (Days)** field, enter the duration in days. If the hold is indefinite, leave this field blank.

7. In the **Note** field, you can enter a note, such as the date and reason for the hold. Be aware that this will appear to the user in Outlook and OWA, so don't add a note here if the user is still active, and you do not want the user to know something is happening.

8. In the **URL:** field, you can enter a URL to an internal site on SharePoint Online or elsewhere with more information about the hold. Again, do not add anything here if you do not want the user to know something is happening.

9. Click **Save**, and then click **Save** again.

It might take up to 60 minutes for the hold to take effect. You can also do this using Power-Shell. To set a hold for one year, use this syntax:

```
set-mailbox mailbox@yourdomain -LitigationHoldEnabled:$true -LitigationHoldDuration 366
```

If you want an unlimited hold, specify the *LitigationHoldDuration* as *Unlimited*. Once the hold is in place, you can remove the license from the user or delete the user object. The mailbox will remain in an inactive state.

Change the hold duration for an inactive mailbox

To change the hold duration, simply use the EAC to change the duration or PowerShell to set a new duration.

Recover an inactive mailbox

You might need to recover an inactive mailbox if the employee who left the organization returns, or if you want to associate an inactive mailbox with a new employee. This process converts the inactive mailbox to a new mailbox associated with a user account, and the inactive mailbox is no more. You must use PowerShell to recover an inactive mailbox. To do this, follow these steps:

1. Connect to Exchange Online using PowerShell.

2. Run this command to list your inactive mailboxes, so you can get the attributes you need to complete this process:

```
Get-Mailbox -InactiveMailboxOnly | FL Name,DistinguishedName,ExchangeGuid,Primary
    SmtpAddress
```

3. Use the *New-Mailbox* command with the *InactiveMailbox* parameter to recover. First, you need to populate a variable with information from the previous command and then create the new mailbox using this command syntax:

```
$InactiveMailbox = Get-Mailbox -InactiveMailboxOnly -Identity <identity of inactive
    mailbox>
New-Mailbox -InactiveMailbox $InactiveMailbox.DistinguishedName -Name
    name -FirstName firstname -LastName lastname -DisplayName "displayname"
    -MicrosoftOnlineServicesID UPN -Password (ConvertTo-SecureString -String
    'P@ssw0rd' -AsPlainText -Force) -ResetPasswordOnNextLogon $true
```

Restore an inactive mailbox

You may might to restore the content of an inactive mailbox if the employee who left the organization returns and you have created a new mailbox for him or her already, or if you want to merge the contents of an inactive mailbox with another mailbox that already exists. This process copies data from the inactive mailbox to another mailbox, and the inactive mailbox remains as is. You must use PowerShell to recover an inactive mailbox. To do this, follow these steps:

1. Connect to Exchange Online using PowerShell.

2. Run this command to list your inactive mailboxes, so you can get the attributes you need to complete this process:

```
Get-Mailbox -InactiveMailboxOnly | FL Name,DistinguishedName,ExchangeGuid,Primary
    SmtpAddress
```

3. You first need to populate a variable with information from the previous command and then create the new mailbox:

```
$InactiveMailbox = Get-Mailbox -InactiveMailboxOnly -Identity <identity of inactive
    mailbox>
```

4. Run this command to restore the content into an existing mailbox, matching existing folders and creating any that do not already exist:

```
New-MailboxRestoreRequest -SourceMailbox $InactiveMailbox.DistinguishedName
    -TargetMailbox newemployee@contoso.com -AllowLegacyDNMismatch
```

5. Run this command to restore the content to a specific top-level folder and create a new folder structure underneath that matches the original mailbox:

```
New-MailboxRestoreRequest -SourceMailbox $InactiveMailbox.DistinguishedName
    -TargetMailbox newemployee@contoso.com -TargetRootFolder "Inactive Mailbox"
    -AllowLegacyDNMismatch
```

EXAM TIP KNOW THE DIFFERENCE BETWEEN RECOVER AND RESTORE

Make sure you know the difference between recovering an inactive mailbox and restoring an inactive mailbox. "Recovering converts, restoring copies" is a straightforward way to remember this because when you restore from backup tapes, you still have the backups.

Delete an inactive mailbox

Before you can delete an inactive mailbox, any holds upon the mailbox or retention policies must either expire or be removed. If all expire, the mailbox will be marked for deletion and removed automatically.

Skill 4.5: Manage search and investigation

Whether from an internal investigation, litigation, or simply because something has been misplaced by a user, finding data will be a component of managing your Office 365 environment. Content search can be handled by administrators or delegated to specific individuals and uses both web-based and command-line tools.

> **In this skill, you learn how to:**
> - Plan for content search and eDiscovery
> - Delegate permissions to use search and discovery tools
> - Use search and investigation tools to perform content searches
> - Export content search results
> - Manage eDiscovery cases

Plan for content search and eDiscovery

Content search and eDiscovery are very similar, and both can be performed from either the Security & Compliance Center or by using PowerShell. Both content searches and eDiscovery can find data throughout Office 365 services. The biggest difference is in how the found data will be used. Content searches are typically ad hoc, where data needs to be found because you are trying to assess the state of things, you are looking for data that might be sensitive or needs protection, or you have a one-off need. You can export the results of the search. Content search queries can be saved to be used again but do not enforce any sort of restrictions or preservation of the data that is found. eDiscovery is most often used for specific requirements and when the results of the search must be preserved, typically in response to a search warrant, discovery motion, or because you wish to pursue legal action and must preserve the results as evidence of wrong-doing. eDiscovery searches and their results are maintained as cases, and you can have separate administrative rights delegated to each case if you need to have multiple users running searches while keeping them out of one another's activities.

In larger organizations, particularly those that are multinational, you might need to establish compliance boundaries so that only certain individuals or teams can search specific locations (specific users' mailboxes, SharePoint sites, and the like) and not all locations. You can read more about how to set up compliance boundaries at *https://docs.microsoft.com/en-us/ microsoft-365/compliance/set-up-compliance-boundaries*.

Delegate permissions to use search and discovery tools

There are two built-in groups in the Security & Compliance Center related to Content Search and eDiscovery. eDiscovery Managers can use both Content Search and eDiscovery and perform all the actions within both for their own searches, but they cannot access cases created by other eDiscovery Managers. eDiscovery Administrators can do everything an eDiscovery Manager can do, can access case data for any Advanced eDiscovery case in the organization, and can add themselves to any eDiscovery case and then manage that case. These two roles are the only two that can preview or export data, and decrypt RMS-encrypted data. In the Security & Compliance Center, both are listed as the eDiscovery Manager role. Open the properties of that role to see or assign the eDiscovery Administrator role to a user.

In addition to these two roles, there are three others that might be involved in Content Search and/or eDiscovery. Compliance Administrators can perform searches and create/manage their own cases and place data on hold. Users in the Organization Management role can do that as well, plus they can perform search and purge actions, and of course, they can add themselves to any of the other roles. The last role is Reviewer, which can review the results of existing cases only.

An Organization Management member or higher can use the Permission panel in the Security & Compliance Center to assign membership to users for other roles.

Use search and investigation tools to perform content searches

Content searches can be performed in the Security & Compliance Center by anyone with the appropriate role membership. To perform a content search, do the following:

1. Log in to the Security & Compliance Center at *https://protection.office.com*.
2. On the left panel, expand **Search** and click **Content Search** to open a new tab.
3. Click the **+New Search** button or the **+Guided Search** button. The only difference is that the Guided Search GUI is more wizard driven, so we will use that for this example.
4. Enter a **Name** and a **Description** for your search and then click **Next**.

5. Select the locations to search. You can select **All Locations**, which will include all Exchange mailboxes and public folders, all SharePoint Online sites, all OneDrive for Business locations, all Office 365 group sites, and all Teams sites. Alternatively, you can select **Specific Locations** and specify which of those you wish to search; also, you can limit your search to specific mailboxes and SharePoint sites. While you can search all locations, the larger the volume of data you have in Office 365, the longer such a search will take. If you can narrow down the locations to search, the search will complete more quickly. Make your selections and then click **Next**.

6. Enter keywords relevant to your search, one word or phrase per line. A search will logically *OR* any words or phrases in the **Keywords** list when conducting a search. If you want to logically *AND* two or more words or phrases, enter them on the same line with an *AND* between them.

7. You can click the **+ Add Conditions** button shown in Figure 4-34 to add things to narrow down the search, such as *Subject* in an email or a *Date* range.

FIGURE 4-34 A content search condition card

When you have your query ready, click **Finish**. The content search will begin as soon as you click Finish. How long it takes depends upon how broad your search is and how much data is within your tenant. Once it completes, you can view the results. If you get no results, as shown in Figure 4-35, you can edit the query in the results pane and re-run the search.

You can view the items that were found, and statistics about the search including the number of locations, the number of items, and the size (see Figure 4-36).

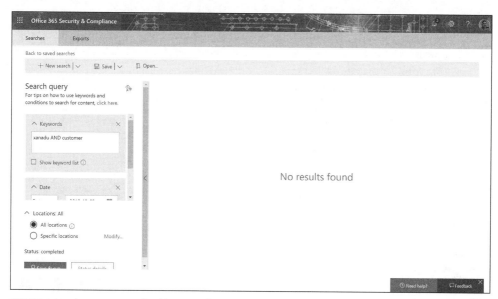

FIGURE 4-35 A content search with no results

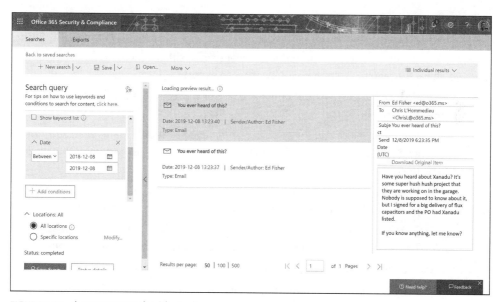

FIGURE 4-36 A content search with results

You can download the original item, or you can click the **Search Statistics** drop-down menu in the upper-right corner to switch from results to statistics to see the number of items searched, the number found, and the size (see Figure 4-37). You can download the statistics as a CSV if desired.

Once you have a search results, you can click the **Save** button to keep the results available for later review.

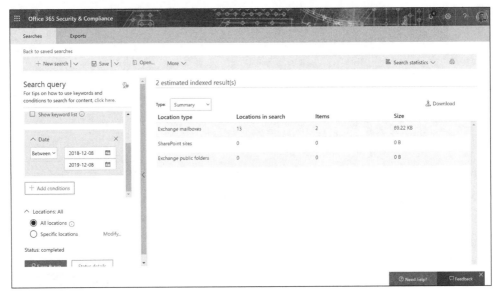

FIGURE 4-37 A content search's statistics

Export content search results

Search results might need to be exported for further review, either by internal or third parties. Once you have the search results, here is how you can export the information:

1. Click the **More** button to export either a report or the results. In this example, we will export the results.

2. Select whether to export only messages that matched the query; items that matched or could not be ruled out due to encryption and so on; or to only export items that could not be ruled out.

3. For Exchange content, select whether to export one PST per mailbox; one PST for all messages; or one PST with one folder for each location containing matches.

4. For Exchange data, you have the option to check the **Deduplication** box to enable deduplication, which reduces the amount of data that exists in multiple locations.

5. For SharePoint data, you can include versions if desired and if versioning was enabled.

6. You also have the option to export files as zipped folders.

7. When you have the desired options set, click **Export**.

8. This will return you to the **Searches** page, where you click the **Exports** tab.

9. If you do not see your export, click the **Refresh** button, and then click your export when it appears.

10. Click **Download Results**. You will be prompted to install the Microsoft Office 365 eDiscovery Export Tool. You need this small download to be able to access the export. The eDiscovery Export Tool will install, and the dialog box shown in Figure 4-38 will appear.

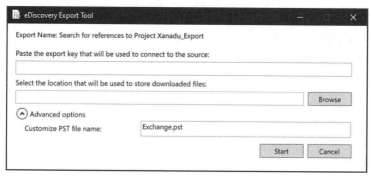

FIGURE 4-38 The eDiscovery Export Tool

11. Go back to the **Export** screen in the Security & Compliance Center. In the **Export Key:** section, click **Copy To Clipboard** to copy the export key, and then paste it into the **Select The Location That Will Be Used To Store Downloaded Files** field in the export tool, which is shown Figure 4-39. Browse to where you want to save the export, and if desired, change the name of the PST.

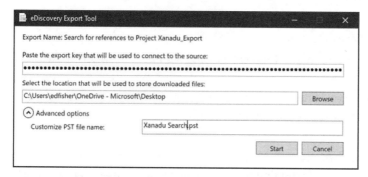

FIGURE 4-39 The eDiscovery Export Tool with all fields completed

12. Click **Start** and wait for the download to complete. The amount of time this takes depends upon the amount of data and your download speed, but you should expect several minutes, even with a small amount of data and a very fast connection. Think lunch break, not coffee break; or you might even need to come back tomorrow.

13. Once the download completes, you can work with the exported data or provide it to others.

REAL WORLD THIS IS GOING TO TAKE SOME TIME

The amount of time it takes for the download of the export to complete is dependent upon the amount of data to download and both the maximum size and concurrent operations limits. See *https://docs.microsoft.com/en-us/microsoft-365/compliance/export-search-results* for more information, tips to increase download speed, and required steps to take if you are trying to access Office 365 through a forward web proxy.

Manage eDiscovery cases

Everything in eDiscovery involves a case. That does not necessarily mean an actual legal case, but nevertheless, we refer to eDiscovery actions as "cases." eDiscovery options that are available to you depend upon your licensing. Standard eDiscovery is available for customers with Office 365 E3 or Microsoft 365 E3 licensing, while Advanced eDiscovery is available with Office 365 E5 or Microsoft 365 E5. Both give you the ability to search for content across all of Office 365, place relevant content on hold, and export the results.

Advanced eDiscovery adds capabilities to this, including the ability to better manage cases, perform search and analytics of the case data, perform near-duplicate detection, thread conversations instead of individual emails, perform OCR on several graphics formats, and evaluate relevance. In addition to making this a much more powerful and specific search, it can greatly reduce the costs of analysis by external council through the deduplication and relevance capabilities. For organizations involved in significant legal activities, that alone can more than offset the additional costs of a full E5 license.

To create and manage an eDiscovery case, do the following:

1. Log in to the Security & Compliance Center at *https://protection.office.com*.

2. In the left panel, click **eDiscovery** > **Advanced eDiscovery**.

3. Click the **Create A Case** button.

4. Enter a **Name** for your case. You can also enter a **Case Number** and **Description** if you like.

5. You can choose to make additional settings now or later. For this example, we will select **Yes** so that we can specify additional settings.

6. Click **Save**.

7. This brings you to the **Settings** tab for your case. You will see additional tabs along the top. You can edit the **Case Information** or even delete the case if necessary. Also, you can add members who can access and manage the case, and you can configure the advanced settings such as deduplication and threading on the **Settings** tab.

8. Click the **Searches** tab and then click the **New Search** button to create a search.

9. Give the search a **Name** and **Description** and then click **Next**.

10. On the next screen, add any custodians you need to include and then click **Next**.

11. Select the locations for searching content. These are the same options as those that are available to you when you are using **Content Search**. Click **Next**.

12. Enter the search criteria. Again, these criteria are the same as those that are available when you are using **Content Search**. When you are done, click **Next**.

13. Review your search and then click **Run**.

14. You will return to the **Searches** tab where you can see that your search is running. You might periodically want to click the **Refresh** button to see when your search is complete (see Figure 4-40).

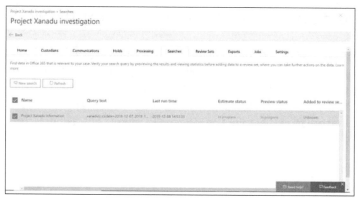

FIGURE 4-40 An Advanced eDiscovery search running

Once the search is complete, you can preview the results by selecting the **Searches** tab. From there, you can preview the results, view statistics, and add the results to a review set. A review set is where you have the collection of search results for further analysis, collaboration, or export:

1. Click the **Review Sets** tab.
2. Select the review set you created for the search.
3. Click the **Action** button and select **Export**.
4. Complete the **Export Options** to export the search results (see Figure 4-41).

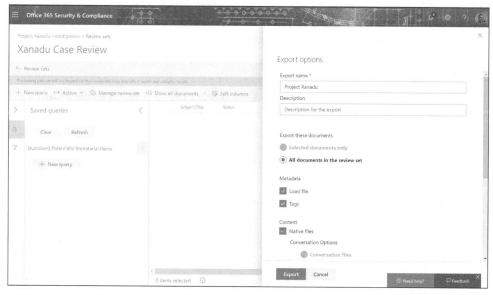

FIGURE 4-41 Exporting an Advanced eDiscovery case

Skill 4.6: Manage data privacy regulation compliance

Compliance with data privacy regulations like the General Data Protection Regulation (GDPR) or the California Consumer Privacy Act (CCPA) are extremely important for organizations, both because it's the right thing to do and because violations of the regulations contained within these and other regulations carry significant financial penalties. There are several other regulatory compliance standards that organizations might be required to comply with, either by law or by contract.

> **In this skill, you learn how to:**
> - Plan for regulatory compliance in Microsoft 365
> - Review and interpret GDPR dashboards and reports
> - Manage Data Subject Requests (DSRs)
> - Review Compliance Manager reports
> - Create and perform Compliance Manager assessments and action items

Plan for regulatory compliance in Microsoft 365

Microsoft Compliance Manager is a tool that administrators can use to track compliance, assign actions to others, and to verify compliance with many different compliance regulations and standards.

> **EXAM TIP**   **THE ONLY CONSTANT IS CHANGE.**
>
> Eventually, the Microsoft Compliance Manager tool will be replaced by Microsoft Compliance Score. The exam blueprint was last updated November 26, 2019, and at the time of this writing, it still calls out Microsoft Compliance Manager, so you want to be familiar with it for the exam. You can read about the new Microsoft Compliance Score at *https://docs.microsoft.com/en-us/microsoft-365/compliance/compliance-score*.

Compliance Manager helps administrators to ensure compliance through several different components:

- Provides customers with access to the reports and results of independent auditors' assessments of Office 365, along with supporting information.
- Gives administrators a place to assign actions to others in their organization, track actions, upload documents, and record compliance with applicable standards.
- Tracks a Compliance Score so that organizations can track their progress toward full compliance with all relevant standards they select.

Skill 4.2 earlier in this chapter covers the Microsoft Compliance Manager tool. In the next section, we will look more closely at things specific to GDPR.

Review and interpret GDPR dashboards and reports

The GDPR Dashboard in the Security & Compliance Center includes tools for administrators to discover, govern, protect, and monitor personal data within their organization. Remember, in this case, personal data refers to any data that can be used to identify an individual. The dashboard includes shortcuts to the GDPR toolbox and to Data subject requests (more on this below). The dashboard also provides visual reporting on cases; data classification; labels; risks and threats; and DLP policy matches. These are the same things we have previously discussed and are available in other areas of the Security & Compliance Center. By collecting them all here, admins can more easily focus on things directly related to GDPR.

To use the GDPR toolbox, do the following:

1. Log in to the Security & Compliance Center at *https://protection.office.com*.

2. In the left panel, expand **Data Privacy** and then click **GDPR Dashboard**.

3. Click the **Open The GDPR Toolbox** shortcut, which is shown in Figure 4-42.

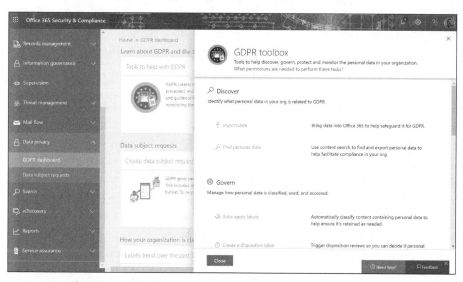

FIGURE 4-42   The GDPR toolbox

The GDPR toolbox includes shortcuts to several actions or tools that are relevant to GDPR. They are grouped as follows:

- **Discover.** This helps you to identify personal data related to GDPR in your organization. It includes shortcuts to Import Data and Content Search so you can find existing personal data.

- **Govern.** This helps you to manage the classification, use, and access of personal data, and includes shortcuts to Labels and Compliance Manager.

- **Protect.** This helps you to secure personal data and detect and respond to threats. It includes shortcuts to DLP and to Office 365 Advanced Threat Protection policies.

- **Monitor And Respond.** The largest section includes what you need to track label usage, respond to DSRs, and conduct investigations. It includes shortcuts to Data Subject Requests, eDiscovery, Labels, Alert Policies, Reporting, and the Service Assurance portal.

Again, while all these tools exist in other locations, centralizing them both makes it easier to focus on GDPR compliance, and highlights their relevance to GDPR compliance.

Manage Data Subject Requests (DSRs)

Data subject requests (DSRs) are requests by individuals, known as data subjects, to an organization, known as the data controller, to take action on data held by the controller and is personal data about the data subject. This might be a request to update data or even delete it. The GDPR provides all residents of the European Union with the legal right to submit DSRs to any organization that holds data about them, regardless of where the organization operates or is incorporated. That means while yours might be an incorporated business operating within the United States, if you have any personal data about a resident of the EU—either because they are a customer or filled out a form on your website—that EU resident can submit a DSR to you, and you must comply with it.

If you receive a DSR, you should create a DSR case. To do that, follow these steps:

1. Log in to the Security & Compliance Center at *https://protection.office.com*.
2. In the left panel, expand **Data Privacy**, and click **Data Subject Requests**.
3. Click the **+ New DSR Case** button.
4. Enter a **Name** and, optionally, a **Description**. When you are done, click **Next**.
5. Enter the name of the person who filed this request. This should be the name as it appears in any personal data. If a data subject goes by more than one variant of his or her name, you will have to modify the search to include variants. Enter the most commonly used variant, then click **Next**.
6. Review the settings, edit if necessary, and then click **Save**.
7. You can immediately run a search if desired by clicking the **Show Me Search Results** button, as shown in Figure 4-43.

FIGURE 4-43 Creating a DSR case

8. **Clicking Show Me Search Results** will open a new tab and run a **Content Search** on all locations, as shown in Figure 4-44.

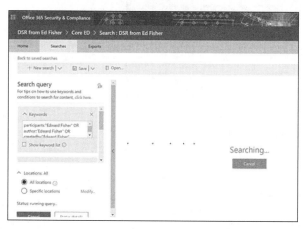

FIGURE 4-44   An in-progress content search for a DSR case

9. You can then export the results if the request is for a copy, or you can take other actions based on the DSR.

While GDPR does provide EU residents with the right to be forgotten, litigation holds or the retention of data necessary to meet other compliance requirements or regulations make take precedence over this. To ensure you meet all obligations, your legal counsel should be involved whenever a request to remove data about a data subject is received.

Review Compliance Manager reports

As mentioned previously, Microsoft has rolled out changes to compliance reports with which the exam has not yet caught up. Compliance Manager reports are accessed through the Compliance Manager tool. You can access this through the Security & Compliance Center in the **Service Assurance** section or directly at *https://aka.ms/compliancemanager*.

To review Compliance Manager reports the "old way," you can do the following:

1. Log in to *https://servicetrust.microsoft.com*.

2. If prompted, authenticate using your Office 365 administrative account credentials.

3. At the top of the page, click **Compliance Manager** and select **Compliance Manager (Classic)**.

4. You can see the assessments already associated with your environment, or you can click the **+Add Assessment** link at the top to add one or more assessments to your portal (see Figure 4-45).

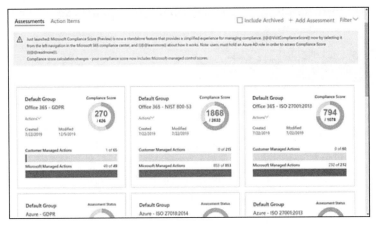

FIGURE 4-45   The classic Compliance Manager dashboard

5. Click the name of an assessment to view details.

6. You will see several sections, including in-scope items, Microsoft Managed Controls, and Customer Managed Controls.

7. Expand the **Customer Managed Controls** section, and you will see the sections and controls relevant to the compliance standard. You can manage documents that you or others have uploaded related to testing and affirmation of a compliance standard, update the status if you are working on one, or assign the control to a user for completion.

Create and perform Compliance Manager assessments and action items

Action items are those things your organization must do to assess and confirm you are in compliance with your responsibilities for any compliance standard. The user who is assigned the item will perform the necessary testing; also, this user can upload supporting documents to the Compliance Manager for storage and update the status as appropriate (see Figure 4-46).

The user will receive an email notification of the assignment that includes a link to the **Compliance Portal**. The user can upload supporting documentation and update the status as appropriate.

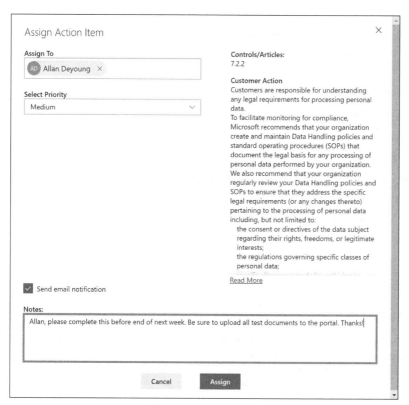

FIGURE 4-46 Assigning an action item in Compliance Manager

Thought Experiment

In the following Thought Experiments, apply what you've learned in this chapter. You can find answers to these questions in the "Thought Experiment answers" section at the end of this chapter.

Configure and analyze security reporting

1. Your organization uses Windows 10 Enterprise. All users are assigned a Microsoft 365 E3 license, and all workstations are managed with Intune. You need to ensure that only security-related data is sent to Microsoft. What level of logging should you enable to accomplish this?

   A. Level 0

   B. Level 1

   C. Level 2

   D. Level 3

2. You want to enable members of your organization's security team to view Secure Score. You do not want them to be able to make any changes. What built-in role should you add their accounts to in order to accomplish this?

   A. Secure Score Users

   B. Security Reader

   C. Security Administrators

   D. View-Only Organization Management

3. You need to be notified immediately if a user attempts to email PII information. What should you do to accomplish this?

   A. Configure an audit policy notification.

   B. Configure an DLP violation notification.

   C. Configure an alert policy.

   D. Add yourself to the DLP Managers group.

Manage and analyze audit logs and reports

1. You need to search the audit logs to determine who modified a security policy setting. Where would you go to do this?

   A. **Reports** > **Administrative Change Log**

   B. **Alerts** > **View Alerts**

   C. **Supervision** > **Administrative Change Log**

   D. **Search** > **Audit log search**

2. You want to receive a notification each time someone creates a new inbox rule. Where would you go to do this?

   A. **Alerts** > **Alert Policies**

   B. **Auditing** > **Alerts**

   C. **Threat Management** > **Alerts**

   D. **Data Loss Prevention** > **Rules** > **Notifications**

3. What is the maximum number of times an alert can be generated by the same event in a 24-hour period?

   A. **One.** Alert summary emails are sent once per day.

   B. **24.** Alerts cannot be sent more than once per hour for the same event.

   C. **3600.** The maximum rate that alerts can be sent is once per minute.

   D. **Unlimited.** You can set No Limit for the daily notification limit.

Configure Office 365 classification and labeling

1. What is personal data?

   A. Data that is created or saved by the user in their OneDrive for Business.

   B. Data that contains personally identifiable information (PII) or that can be used to identify an individual.

   C. Account data used in security questions for self-service password reset.

   D. Data on unmanaged mobile devices which is outside the scope of mobile application management policies.

2. What do you designate data that must be saved and cannot be changed during the time it is saved?

   A. Immutable

   B. Litigation Hold

   C. Record

   D. Static

3. Which of the following cannot be accomplished with retention?

   A. Maintain copies of edited documents.

   B. Retain data and prevent it from being deleted.

   C. Delete data.

   D. Move data to archive.

Manage data governance and retention

1. Which license type is eligible for converting a mailbox to inactive?

   A. Exchange Online Plan 1

   B. Exchange Online Archiving

   C. Office 365 F1

   D. Inactive Mailbox License

2. You wish to copy data from an inactive mailbox to an existing user's mailbox, maintaining the data they already have in that mailbox. What do you need to do?

   A. Recover an inactive mailbox.

   B. Run a *New-MailboxExport* request.

   C. Restore an inactive mailbox.

   D. Run an eDiscovery search, export the data to PST, and import the PST to the user's mailbox.

3. If you need a user to review a percentage of communications to ensure compliance, what would you use?

   A. Arbitration

   B. Compliance Review

   C. Information Protection

   D. Supervision

Manage search and investigation

1. You need to find all emails between any of your employees and an external company and provide them to your corporate attorney for review. You want to minimize the amount of data, including duplicates, and include all emails in a thread in a single message rather than in individual messages. What option should you use to obtain the data?

   A. Run a content search with the **Minimize Output Size** option.

   B. Use Advanced eDiscovery.

   C. Create a forwarding rule to a Discovery Mailbox and run it against all mailboxes.

   D. Use the *New-MailboxExport* command with the *-Deduplication:$Enabled* option.

2. To what format can you export mail using content search?

   A. *.EML

   B. *.RTF

   C. *.OST

   D. *.PST

3. What do you call the search parameters in eDiscovery?

   A. A case

   B. A matter

   C. An investigation

   D. An inquiry

Manage data privacy regulation compliance

1. What is a Data Subject Request?

   A. A request for audit log information for all access to specific data.

   B. A request from an individual for data about them.

   C. A method for requesting access to data through an API.

   D. A process to request data be designated as a record.

2. What would you use to view compliance reports for security baselines?

 A. Compliance Manager

 B. Auditing

 C. Secure Score

 D. GDPR toolbox

3. Where would you assign compliance-related tasks to another user?

 A. Security & Compliance Center > Roles

 B. Compliance Manager

 C. Security & Compliance Center > Permissions

 D. The GDPR Toolbox > Assignments

Thought Experiment Answers

This section contains the solutions to the thought experiments and answers to the review questions in this chapter.

Configure and analyze security reporting

1. The correct answer is A.
2. The correct answer is B.
3. The correct answer is C.

Manage and analyze audit logs and reports

1. The correct answer is D.
2. The correct answer is A.
3. The correct answer is D.

Configure Office 365 classification and labeling

1. The correct answer is B.
2. The correct answer is C.
3. The correct answer is A.

Manage data governance and retention

1. The correct answer is B.

2. The correct answer is C.

3. The correct answer is D.

Manage search and investigation

1. The correct answer is B.

2. The correct answer is D.

3. The correct answer is A.

Manage data privacy regulation compliance

1. The correct answer is B.

2. The correct answer is A.

3. The correct answer is B.

Index

A

D

J–K–L

M

Q

R

Plug into learning at

MicrosoftPressStore.com

The Microsoft Press Store by Pearson offers:

- Free U.S. shipping

- Buy an eBook, get three formats – Includes PDF, EPUB, and MOBI to use with your computer, tablet, and mobile devices

- Print & eBook Best Value Packs

- eBook Deal of the Week – Save up to 50% on featured title

- Newsletter – Be the first to hear about new releases, announcements, special offers, and more

- Register your book – Find companion files, errata, and product updates, plus receive a special coupon* to save on your next purchase

 Pearson